BUS & COACH
RECOGNITION

ALAN MILLAR

IAN ALLAN Publishing

First published 1992

ISBN 0 7110 2060 4

Published by Ian Allan Ltd, Shepperton, Surrey;
and printed by Ian Allan Printing Ltd at their
works at Coombelands in Runnymede,
England.

Cover:
Optare's Spectra, the long-awaited DAF-bodied
replacement for the MCW Metrobus.
Andrew Jarosz

Back cover top:
A Reeve Burgess-bodied Mercedes-Benz 709D
in Badgerline's latest livery.

Back cover bottom:
The prototype Plaxton Excalibur body,
Plaxton's high-floor flagship body introduced
for the 1992 season, on a Volvo B10M
chassis. *Both: Stephen Morris*

CONTENTS

PART 1
DOUBLE-DECK BUSES

PART 2
SINGLE-DECK BUSES

Bodywork

PART 3
COACHES

Bus chassis also used as coaches
Chassis built exclusively as coaches
Coach bodies and integrals

PART 4
MINIBUSES

Chassis and base vans

Bodies and complete vehicles

INTRODUCTION

The range of buses and coaches on UK roads has, if anything, grown in the four years since the second edition of *Bus & Coach Recognition* was published. Continued low investment, a consequence of privatisation and economic recession, has meant many older vehicles are being kept longer than before. But manufacturers have been introducing new models ready for a recovery.

Just as the operating industry is changing, with the Stagecoach, Badgerline, Drawlane Transport and Caldaire groups emerging from National Bus Company and Scottish Bus Group privatisation as potentially powerful buyers of new buses, and more municipal companies and London Buses head for privatisation, so there have been radical changes by manufacturers preparing for the post-1992 single European market.

Volvo, which bought Leyland Bus in 1988, bought 75% of Steyr Bus in Austria in 1990 and as part of a far-reaching co-operation deal, Volvo and Renault have taken 45% stakes in each other's bus and truck businesses. In the medium term, they expect to share major components and research and development; long-term, they might merge. The two companies now own 75% of Heuliez Bus, another French bus builder.

United Bus was created in the Netherlands in 1989 to take over DAF Bus and Bova. It has since acquired Optare in the UK, Dutch bodybuilder Den Oudsten and DAB, the one-time Leyland subsidiary in Denmark. Iveco and Mercedes-Benz, giants of the European commercial vehicle industry, want to break into the UK big bus market.

Plaxton has expanded at home, buying most of Duple from Trinity Holdings, minibus builder Mellor; it also bought Iveco's French bodybuilding subsidiary, Carrosserie Lorraine, but has since closed it. It has invested millions in new coach and bus bodies for UK and European markets.

There have been casualties, too. As well as Duple, Metro-Cammell Weymann closed in 1989, with Optare acquiring the rights to its products. Volvo closed its giant Workington plant in 1992 and pulled out of UK bodybuilding. And as demand for new minibuses has slowed and purpose-built midis like the Dennis Dart and Volvo B6R take a larger slice of new bus orders, newer bodybuilders have come and gone. Robin Hood and most of its successor businesses and Carlyle are notable victims. Even Northern Counties, long established in big bus building, was in administrative receivership in 1991.

To reflect this changing scene, there is more space in this edition to help identify small buses and with mid- and front-engined single-deckers, the emphasis is on body identification where chassis features are largely hidden. Data tables continue to provide basic information on each type and show some (not necessarily all) places where local service buses may be found. Inevitably, space prevents the inclusion of every single type of bus and coach on the roads today, but your comments on how to improve *Bus & Coach Recognition* are always welcome. Details to the Publishing Editor, c/o Ian Allan, Terminal House, Station Approach, Shepperton, Surrey TW17 8AS.

The following notes may help make sense of terms used in the book:

How is a bus built? Traditionally, buses and coaches had a separate **chassis** and **body**. The chassis, the frame in which engine, gearbox, axles and wheels are mounted, was built in one factory; the body, all the upper structure in which passengers travel, was fitted in another factory. **Integral** or **chassis-less** construction is more common now, with the body and chassis being a single structure in which mechanical units are mounted. **Semi-integral** designs are a halfway house, with a separate **underframe** for the mechanical units, but depending on the body to bear some of the strength.

Engines are mounted either **vertically** or **horizontally.** Vertical engines are mounted either longitudinally (from front to back in line with the length of the chassis) at the front, in the middle under the floor (hence, **underfloor** engine) or at the rear; or **transversely** (across the width of the chassis) at the rear. **Transmissions**, the gearbox and its method of control by the driver, are either **manual** (clutch and floor-mounted gearlever like most cars), **automatic** (two pedals and switch or push-button control) or **semi-automatic** (two pedals and ability to select all gears). Most manual gearboxes are **synchromesh.**

Bus or coach? A **bus** is designed for local services. Its seats are more robust than luxurious, its doors may be wider, its floor may be nearer the ground and there will be provision for some standing passengers. A **coach** is a more luxurious vehicle for longer journeys, possibly with reclining seats, toilet, galley and larger windows. **Dual purpose** vehicles or **semi-coaches** usually look like buses from the outside but have coach features inside.

Dimensions are governed by Construction and Use regulations. The maximum permitted width is 2.5m (8ft 2½in), maximum length 12m (39ft 4in) on rigid vehicles and 18m (59ft) on articulated buses. Two-axle vehicles are limited to a gross weight (vehicle, passengers and luggage) of 17 tonnes. The most common sizes of buses today reflect former upper limits of lengths and widths. Double-deckers grew from 27ft to 30ft in the mid-1950s, then to 9.5m, 10m, 11m and 12m. Single-deck buses and coaches range from 8.5m to 12m, with 12m the most common length of coaches.

Minibuses, most converted from vans, seat up to around 20 passengers. **Midibuses** bridge the gap to 10m single-deckers.

Double-deckers are either **highbridge** (around 14ft 6in, maybe taller) or **lowheight** (around 13ft 8in to fit under low bridges). Single-deck coaches range between 3m and 3.7m; double-deck coaches are either 4m (for international work) or 4.2m There also are 4m **half-deck** coaches with a lower saloon at the rear.

Body descriptions: Passenger doors are **front** entrances where fitted ahead of the front axle, **forward** entrances when directly behind the front axle and **dual doored** where there are separate entrances and exits. Most buses have two, three or four-leaf folding doors, coaches either have hinged doors or **plug** doors which open to lie with the inner section against the body side and close to seal out draughts. Some coaches have extra offside **Continental** doors for kerbside access in mainland Europe and **peage** windows on the nearside door, so Continental motorway tolls may be paid without opening the door.

Side windows either have **direct glazing** (fixed by adhesive) or **gasket glazing** (fixed by rubber section). **Windscreens** are either **curved** or **flat**. Curved windscreens, if curved in one plane only, are **barrel**-shaped if the curve is from top to bottom; if curved in two planes, they are **double-curvature**. **Vee-shaped** screens use two flat panes set at an angle. **BET** companies pioneered a double-curvature windscreen in the 1960s which remains popular today.

The term **window bays** for side windows may confuse. On double-deckers, convention has it that this refers to the number of lower deck windows, excluding central doors, staircase panels or front and rear overhang. So, a bus with six windows on the upper deck has a four-bay body. On single-deckers, it refers to the number of windows behind the driver's cab.

All pictures are by the author except where stated otherwise.

PART 1 DOUBLE-DECK BUSES

CHASSIS AND INTEGRALS — FRONT-ENGINED

Before 1958, all production double-deck buses for the UK market had front engines mounted over the front axle, to the nearside of the driver, and had provision for the entrance/exit to be on the overhang behind the rear axle. Few remain outside London and the newer Volvo Ailsa, designed as a reaction against the problems of the first generation of rear-engined designs, is beginning to disappear, too.

AEC Routemaster

Built: Southall, Middlesex 1958-68.
Engines: AEC AV590, AV690; Leyland O.600; Cummins C-Series; Iveco 8360; DAF 11.6 litre.

Below:
AEC Routemaster: A standard 64-seat ex-London Transport RM-type with East Yorkshire in Hull. It still has LT destination screens, including a route number box visible behind the nearside mirror, and has wind-down front and side windows. The earliest Routemasters had non-opening front windows.

Above left:
AEC Routemaster: Rear view of a 72-seat London RML, showing the open rear platform and black used ticket box, once familiar on buses in all parts of Britain. Note the extra half bay in the middle, a feature of all 30ft Routemasters.

Left:
AEC Routemaster: A former BEA 56-seat forward entrance RMA-type coach in London Buses' East London fleet. Note the twin headlamps. These buses have more powerful AV690 engines.

Above:
AEC Routemaster: One of London Coaches' 10 ERM-class 76-seat open-toppers created by adding an extra bay to standard RM buses. Note the very long wheelbase.

Transmission: AEC fully and semi-automatic.
Bodywork: Park Royal.
Areas of operation: London, Glasgow, Blackpool, Southend, Hull, Bedford.
The Routemaster is the last traditional double-decker running in any significant number and is expected to survive to the end of the century. It was designed for London Transport and incorporated such advanced features for its day as integral construction, aluminium alloy body, independent front suspension and hydraulic brakes. Of the 2,875 built, most were for LT and over 700 were still running in 1992. Over 400 of the London buses had their worn-out AEC and Leyland engines replaced by Cummins and Iveco engines in 1990/91 and a body refurbishment programme has begun. One London vehicle was re-powered by DAF.

They were built in two lengths, 27ft 6in and 30ft, mostly with rear-entrances, but British European Airways (BEA) and Northern General Transport (Go-Ahead Northern today) bought forward-entrance versions. London fitted platform doors on 112 rear-entrance Green Line semi-coaches. The most common survivors in London are 72-seat RML-class and 64-seat RM-class, but there also are 57-seat RMC ex-Green Line, 56-seat RMA ex-BEA and 65-seat RCL ex-Green Line buses. Added to all that, a new Routemaster class, ERM, was created in 1990 when 10 open-top RMs were lengthened to 32ft 6in with 76 seats; the object is to carry more tourists on the top deck.

The most distinguishing feature is the low bonnet and grille, designed to give the driver a good view of the kerbside. The grille is divided vertically, with space for a triangular AEC/LT

9

badge at the top. The basic body is four-bay, with equal length windows; 30ft models have an extra, shorter window halfway along both decks; the 10 32ft 6in lengthened buses have five-bay bodies. London Routemasters all have wind down windows (most also having them on the top deck front windscreens); the Northern buses had sliding windows. The ex-Green Line buses have additional moulding lines around their windows.

Ex-London Routemasters are operated by Kelvin Central, Blackpool Transport, Southend Transport, East Yorkshire and United Counties on routes where they still justify the employment of bus conductors.

Volvo Ailsa B55

Built: Irvine, Ayrshire 1973-84.
Engine: Volvo TD70.
Transmission: Self-Changing Gears semi- and fully-automatic; Allison and Voith automatic.
Bodywork: Alexander, Van Hool-McArdle, East Lancs, Northern Counties, Marshall.
Areas of operation: Glasgow, Dundee, Fife, Ayrshire, Merseyside, Derby, Cardiff, Leeds.
The Scottish-designed Ailsa was developed when traditional front-engined double-deckers went out of production and some operators found rear-engined designs unreliable. Its semi-integral underframe has a compact, but powerful 6.7-litre engine fitted on the front overhang between the driver's cab and the entrance door. On most, the staircase runs forward from behind the cab, leaving space for only one seat at the front of the top deck. Most Ailsas are 9.8m long with up to 79 seats, but Tayside has 10.3m 84-seaters.

Principal identification points are a three-leaf entrance door (designed to clear the space around the engine compartment), an offside cab door (either hinged or sliding) and a large front radiator grille which hinges up for engine access.

Below:
Volvo Ailsa B55: The offside cab door is a key identification feature of the Ailsa, as is the large lift-up grille. This vehicle, with Black Prince of Morley, is a former South Yorkshire bus with **Van Hool-McArdle** body built in Dublin. Only 65 of these bodies were built for the UK, 64 of which were on Ailsas. *Michael Fowler*

CHASSIS — MID-ENGINED

Horizontal underfloor-engined double-deckers never passed beyond the prototype stage until 1982, when Volvo proved the concept was possible. Compared with rear-engined designs, they offer better weight distribution, a simpler driveline and higher seating capacity, but they are taller.

Leyland Lion

Built: Silkeborg, Denmark 1986-88.
Engine: Leyland TL11H.
Transmission: ZF automatic.
Bodywork: Alexander, East Lancs, Northern Counties.
Areas of operation: Nottingham, Edinburgh, Glasgow.
The Lion was Leyland's answer to Volvo's Citybus. It was developed from the standard single-deck underframe produced by DAB, Leyland's then subsidiary in Denmark, and was withdrawn from the market after Volvo bought Leyland. Only 32 were built, 19 with Alexander bodies for SMT and Clydeside, 13 for Nottingham. It has a front radiator and has a higher floor than the Volvo.

Below:
Leyland Lion: The lines of the **Alexander R-type** body of this Clydeside bus betray the high floor of the Lion. Engine access is by side flaps.

Above:
Volvo Citybus: A Strathclyde Buses Citybus with **Alexander R-type** body with a lower front dash design unique to the operator. Although higher than on rear-engined buses, the Citybus has a lower floor than the Lion.

Volvo Citybus

Built: Irvine, Ayrshire 1982-86; Boras, Sweden 1987 to date.
Chassis: Volvo THD100, 101.
Transmission: Voith or ZF automatic.
Bodywork: Alexander, East Lancs, Marshall, Northern Counties.
Areas of operation: London, Manchester, Liverpool, Glasgow, Edinburgh, Bournemouth, Derby, Northampton, Nottingham, Plymouth, Weston-super-Mare, Burnley, Cambridge, Great Yarmouth.

The replacement for the Ailsa was the British-developed Citybus, variously designated B10MD or D10M, a combination of the mid-underfloor engined B10M coach's running units with a perimeter underframe similar to that used on the Ailsa. As well as reducing the number of unique parts for its double-decker, Volvo also attracted a wider customer base. Like the Lion, it has a front radiator, sometimes concealed behind an Ailsa-size grille and, just to confuse the unwary, some East-Lancs-bodied Citybuses have offside cab doors like the Ailsa.

CHASSIS AND INTEGRALS — REAR-ENGINED

The advent of the Leyland Atlantean, in production from 1958, changed the shape of the British double-decker. Its transverse-mounted rear engine layout has increasingly become the norm and from 1969, when the last old generation of front-engined chassis went out of production, has only been challenged by the Ailsa, the Citybus and Lion and by occasional attempts to sell longitudinally-mounted rear engines.

Bristol VRT

Built: Bristol 1968-81.
Engines: Gardner 6LX, 6LXB, 6LXC; Leyland 501, 680.
Transmission: Self-Changing Gears semi- and fully-automatic.
Bodywork: ECW, Alexander, East Lancs, Northern Counties, Willowbrook.
Areas of operation: Throughout Britain (municipal customers include Great Yarmouth, and Northampton).
The Bristol VRT was the last of the first generation of rear-engined double-deckers to be launched and was developed primarily for the state-owned sector which, until three years earlier, was the only group of operators Bristol was permitted to supply. Many of the 4,500-plus built are operated by former NBC fleets and most are 9.5m long.

They have front radiators. The engine compartment is designed to be enclosed entirely by the bodywork, but East Lancs and MCW bodied some Sheffield, Merseyside and West Midlands vehicles with the same cutaway 'bustle' effect more common on Leyland Atlanteans and Daimler Fleetlines. Models built until 1974 (Series 1 and 2) have cooling vents around the engine compartment; Series 3 models built from then all have enclosed engine compartments with cooling vents located to the rear of the bodywork, below the upper deck windows.

Below:
Bristol VRT: Rear view of Eastern Counties VRTs with **ECW** bodies, showing the difference between Series 3, on the left with enclosed engine compartment and cooling vent in the upper panels, and Series 2 with grilles on the engine compartment.

Daimler (Leyland) Fleetline

Built: Coventry, 1960-73; Leyland, Lancashire 1973-80.
Engines: Gardner 6LX, 6LXB; Leyland 680, 690; Iveco 8361.
Transmission: Self-Changing Gears semi- and fully-automatic.
Bodywork: Alexander, East Lancs, ECW, MCW, Northern Counties, Park Royal, Roe, Willowbrook.
Areas of operation: Throughout Britain (notably West Midlands, Glasgow, Edinburgh, Manchester, Liverpool, London, Derby, Leicester, Teesside).
The second of the first generation and the first built to carry lowheight bodywork, the Fleetline sold to all classes of operator. London Transport alone bought 2,646 in 1970-78, selling most of them in the early 1980s, and many Fleetlines are now operating with second or subsequent owners. Most of those built from the end of 1974 are badged as Leylands.

Below:
Leyland Fleetline: Rear view of a **Northern Counties**-bodied Fleetline in the Cleveland Transit fleet, showing the engine cover with lift-up centre section and offside vertically-slatted radiator grille.

All have their radiator in the engine compartment. Most have it on the offside, behind a vertically slatted grille, in an engine cover with a single opening section for engine access. They have bustle cutaway-effect bodywork above the engine compartment, but some — including the first 2,246 London buses — have side fairings which reduce the cutaway to the area above the centre of the engine cover. The last 400 London Fleetlines, coded B20 by Leyland, were designed to be quieter and are identifiable by a completely different engine cover design, with two sloping ventilator chimneys above the engine — that on the offside being wider. Of these, 200 have had their Leyland 690 engines replaced by Italian-built Iveco diesels and have an additional nearside grille. Many have been withdrawn from London service.

Above:
Leyland Fleetline B20: Rear view of a **Park Royal**-bodied B20 in London Buses' London General fleet, showing the large cooling chimneys and the nearside grille which betrays its Iveco engine. The front of one of these buses, with barrel windscreen, is visible on the right.

15

Iveco TurboCity: The prototype TurboCity double-decker with Italian windscreen, quarterlights and lower dash grafted on to a modified **Alexander R-type** body.
Iveco Ford Truck

Dennis Dominator

Built: Guildford, Surrey 1977 to date.
Engines: Gardner 6LXB, 5LXC, 6LXCT, LG1200; Rolls-Royce (Perkins) Eagle; DAF; Cummins L10.
Transmission: Voith, ZF or Maxwell fully-automatic.
Bodywork: Alexander, East Lancs, Marshall, Northern Counties, Willowbrook.
Areas of operation: South Yorkshire, London, Brighton, Bournemouth, Chester, Eastbourne, Glasgow, Hull, Leicester, Manchester, Swindon, Warrington, Grimsby; also Darlington (single-deck).
A third generation rear-engined double-decker, the Dominator was Dennis's first UK bus chassis for 10 years and has been bought in particular by municipal companies, South Yorkshire Transport, the Drawlane Transport group and by Capital Citybus in London. It is also exported to the Far East. East Lancs and Marshall bodied 33 11m single-deck Dominators in 1978-80, most of which remain in service in Chester and Darlington. The Dominator has a front-mounted radiator, provision for the engine compartment to be fully enclosed — where it is not, thick body panels are required to conceal engine cooling ducts — and it has cooling grilles at the sides, directly above the engine compartment.

Iveco TurboCity

Built: Valle Uffita, Italy 1991 to date.
Engine: Iveco 8460.21.
Transmission: ZF automatic.
Bodywork: Alexander.
As part of a long term plan to sell full-size buses in the UK, Iveco — Fiat's commercial vehicle group — launched the TurboCity 100, a 10.7m double-deck version of its TurboCity-U single-decker in 1991. It was to be followed in 1992 by 10.7m and 11.9m single-deckers designated TurboCity 50. The numbers approximate to their seating capacities, although axle load limits restrict the double-decker to 83 seats, despite it being longer than its competitors. The chassis has air suspension, independent at the front. The Alexander body is a variant of its R-type design, with Italian single-piece windscreens and deep quarterlights grafted on to the front. The lower-deck back window is omitted.

Leyland Atlantean

Built: Leyland, Lancashire 1958-84.
Engines: Leyland O.600, 680, 690.
Transmission: Leyland semi- and fully-automatic; Voith automatic.
Bodywork: Alexander, East Lancs, ECW, MCW, Marshall, Northern Counties, Park Royal, Roe, Van Hool-McArdle, Willowbrook.
Areas of operation: Throughout UK (notably Glasgow, Edinburgh, Newcastle, Manchester, Liverpool, Sheffield, Leeds, Nottingham, Southampton, Preston, Hull, Isle of Man).

All classes of operator bought the Atlantean over its long production run and it is still a common sight on the streets of larger cities, especially in Greater Manchester and Merseyside where some of the last were supplied. There are still a few PDR1 and PDR2 models built before the later AN68 variant was introduced in 1972. Where these retain their original bonnet assemblies, they have an offside radiator grille with vertical louvres and later models have a nearside grille, too. Most have three-piece engine covers, the centre section of

Below:
Leyland Atlantean: A Yorkshire Rider Atlantean AN68 with **Roe** body. Note the mouldings for a nearside grille and the cooling vents on the top of the engine cover. This also shows how engine fairings can be used to disguise the rear bustle.

which lifts up and the outer (offside and nearside) sections hinge outwards; on pre-1962 models, the entire bonnet assembly lifts up. The AN68 has a redesigned engine cover with larger meshed grilles and a more substantial mock bumper around the bottom of the engine compartment; from 1975, nearside grilles were deleted and a blank moulding used instead. But beware of possible confusion. Some late PDR1s were supplied with AN68 engine covers and other buses have been modified on overhaul. And Cleveland Transit fitted Fleetline engine covers on some of its Atlanteans, some of which are now operated by East Yorkshire.

Some Atlanteans have engine fairings which extend to the centre section of the bonnet. Fishwick of Leyland has two prototype AN69 chassis with turbocharged 690 engines; one has the same 'quiet pack' engine covers as London's B20 Fleetlines.

Leyland Titan

Built: Park Royal, West London 1978-80 (prototypes built 1975-77), Workington, Cumbria 1981-84.
Engines: Gardner 6LXB, 6LXCT, Leyland TL11 (501 in prototypes).
Transmission: Leyland fully-automatic.
Height: High.
Areas of operation: London, Reading, Swindon, Preston.

The Titan was meant to be Leyland's standard double-decker for the 1980s. It was developed in the early 1970s using lessons learned from the first generation of rear-engined double-deckers and, like the Routemaster, was bestowed with features requested by London Transport. It came with integral construction, independent front suspension, hydraulic brakes and, to achieve better engine cooling, a separately located radiator compartment above the engine. It took longer than planned to put it into production and even then fewer were built than planned. In the end, London and Reading were its only long-term customers, London buying 1,164 new and five secondhand from West Midlands and Reading took 12, 10 of them with Gardner 6LXCT engines. The only other batch of significance, 15 for Greater Manchester, was sold in the mid-1980s and five of these operate with Swindon & District. The London fleet now has air brakes instead of hydraulic.

Below:
Leyland Titan: Front and rear views of London Buses Titans, showing the tall lower deck windows and the asymmetric rear end with large radiator compartment.

Titans have straight-sided bodies which taper inwards from the base of the upper deck windows. Lower saloon headroom, at 1.9m, is the best for any British double-decker and the Titan has particularly tall lower deck windows. The driver's windscreen is of the barrel-shaped design standardised by London Transport. They are most distinguishable at the back by the asymmetric window arrangement above the engine compartment. The lower saloon rear window (with stick-on wide angle visor) is offset within shrouds and is level with the front of the engine compartment; the offside area above the engine is occupied by the radiator.

Leyland Olympian

Built: Bristol 1978-83; Workington, Cumbria 1983-92; Irvine, Ayrshire from 1992.
Engines: Gardner 6LXB, 6LXCT, 5LXCT, LG1200; Leyland TL11; Cummins L10.
Transmission: Leyland semi- or fully-automatic, Voith, ZF, Maxwell automatic.
Bodywork: Leyland, Alexander, East Lancs, ECW, Marshall, Northern Counties, Optare, Roe.
Areas of operation: Throughout Britain (notably London, Edinburgh, Glasgow, Aberdeen, Newcastle, Liverpool, Manchester, Leeds, Bristol, Cardiff, Preston, Derby, Nottingham, Birmingham, Swindon, Salisbury, Bournemouth, Oxford, Luton, Reading, Cambridge, Norwich, Southend, Isle of Wight, Isle of Man).

Although conceived as a lowheight version of the Titan, to be supplied to customers of independent bodybuilders which might not otherwise buy a Leyland, the Olympian became its standard double-decker and is reckoned now to be the world's best-selling double-decker. It has a less sophisticated air suspension, air brakes and a simpler cooling system with a front-mounted radiator. The engine compartment, to which there are cooling ducts from the rear of the upper deck sides, is totally enclosed on most buses or within thick body sides as on some Dennis Dominators. It is built in 9.6m, 10m, 11m and three-axle 12m form; to date, only the Stagecoach group has taken three 12m models in the UK. Most Olympians are now built with the Cummins/ZF driveline.

Below:
Leyland Olympian: Rear view of a lowheight **ECW**-bodied Olympian operated by Midland Fox.

MCW Metropolitan

Built: Birmingham, 1973-78.
Engine: Scania D11.
Transmission: Scania automatic.
Height: High.
Areas of operation: Leicester, Cambridge.

The Metropolitan is a product of a joint venture by which Metro-Cammell Weymann, previously an independent bodybuilder, built integral buses based on Swedish-built Scania running units. The Metro-Scania single-decker had been introduced in 1969 and was followed in 1973 by the Metropolitan, a second generation challenge to British Leyland's monopoly of the double-deck market. The underframe is adapted from the Scania BR111 single-decker of 1972 and introduced air suspension, torque converter transmission and encapsulated quiet engines to a market used to less sophisticated Leyland products. The bodywork is similar to standard bodywork built at the time by MCW, with the generally square body tapering in from the upper deck windows. But it differs by having a barrel-shaped driver's windscreen of asymmetric design, with deeper nearside glazing to give the driver better kerbside visibility, a thick chrome beading strip around the base of the lower deck windows and a totally enclosed engine compartment with glazing carried on to the end of the lower deck sides. The rear is distinguished by an air intake pod effect on the roof and mouldings which conceal cooling ducts from the roof to the engine compartment. There are two radiators, one on either side ahead of the rear axle.

In total, 660 were built for the British market, but corrosion and gearbox problems cut short the lives of most. The last significant Metropolitan operators are Leicester Citybus and Whippet Coaches.

Below:
MCW Metropolitan: An ex-London Metropolitan operated by Whippet Coaches in Cambridge. The staircase is towards the centre as it originally had a central exit door.

MCW Metrobus

Built: Birmingham, 1978-89.
Engines: Gardner 6LXB, Rolls-Royce Eagle, Cummins L10.
Transmission: Voith automatic.
Bodywork: MCW, Alexander, Northern Counties.
Height: High and semi-low.
Areas of operation: London, West Midlands, Glasgow, Newcastle, Liverpool, Manchester, West Yorkshire, Bristol, Hull, Leicester, Reading, Canterbury, Burton upon Trent, Barnsley.
The Metropolitan was succeeded by the Metrobus, the first complete bus to be designed and built by MCW. The chassis and engines were British, the gearbox a German unit fast gaining customers among UK operators. MCW's courage in launching it with little development was rewarded by healthy initial orders, especially after Leyland suspended Titan production in 1980/81. London bought over 1,400 and West Midlands over 1,100.

In its initial form, the highbridge MCW bodywork (with which most were fitted) is derived from the Metropolitan, but with lessons learned from the older model's corrosion problems. It is a slightly squarer shape without the mouldings added to the Metropolitan; the asymmetric windscreen is retained, but is slightly shallower; the radiator is in the engine compartment, on the offside, but there also is a front grille, painted black on earlier models, less elaborate later; and the engine compartment has no glazing directly above the sides of the engine. Most of the London Metrobuses are to this design.

The Mk 2 body was launched in 1982. It has 60% fewer body parts and was cheaper to build. It differs most markedly at the front, where it has a peaked roof dome, a shallower symmetrical driver's windscreen with either barrel-shaped or flat glass and more heavily moulded front panels and grille. The pillars between the side windows are slightly wider and it has a much larger glass area on the upper deck rear emergency door.

Metrobus underframes were also bodied by Alexander, in highbridge and semi-lowheight form, and by Northern Counties for Greater Manchester. For details of these, see the respective bodybuilders' sections.

Above:
MCW Metrobus: Front and rear views of Mk 1 Metrobuses in the Stevensons fleet. The one on the left is ex-West Midlands, the other ex-South Yorkshire.

Above:
MCW Metrobus: A Mk 2 Metrobus operated by Yorkshire Rider. It has a barrel-shaped windscreen.

Below:
Optare Spectra: The first Spectra, for Reading Transport, was launched at the 1991 Coach & Bus Show in Birmingham. Engine cooling is by grilles on the engine compartment.

Optare Spectra

Built: Leeds, West Yorkshire and Eindhoven, Netherlands 1991 to date.
Engine: DAF 9 litre.
Transmission: ZF or Voith automatic.
Height: High and low.
Areas of operation: Reading, London.

The Spectra is a reincarnation of the Metrobus. After MCW closed in 1989, Optare and DAF bought the rights to the design and jointly developed what some suggest might be the last entirely new double-decker for the UK market. Its 10m DAF DB250 chassis uses the rear axle and suspension of the Metrobus and has a transverse engine, but it shares many chassis parts with the SB220 single-decker. The body, available in 13ft 8in and 14ft 2in form, is built using the Alusuisse system of interlocking aluminium extrusions and is an entirely new product with large front windscreens and side windows similar to those on Optare single-deckers. Like the Iveco, it has no lower deck back window, just a space on which operators can place advertisements.

Scania N112/N113

Built: Katrineholm, Sweden 1980 to date.
Engines: Scania DS11.
Transmission: Voith or Scania automatic.
Bodywork: Alexander, Northern Counties, East Lancs, Marshall.
Areas of operation: London, Newcastle, Nottingham, Greater Manchester, Liverpool, Newport, Brighton, West Yorkshire, Birmingham, Cardiff, Hull, Maidstone.

After MCW severed its ties with Scania to develop the Metrobus, Scania developed a successor double-decker for the UK. This used the running units of the CR112 single-decker of 1978, but with a chassis frame designed to take low-floor double-deck bodies. In light of the Metropolitan experience, Voith gearboxes were offered as standard in the early days, as

Below:
Scania N112: The offside grille, ahead of the rear axle, is a key feature of the Scania N-Series. This also shows the rear end treatment of **East Lancs** Alexander-style bodies.

an option more recently, and the cooling arrangement was simplified to one radiator, mounted ahead of the offside rear wheel. The engine compartment remained enclosed, as on the Metropolitan. The chassis, which is also built as an 11.2m single-decker, began life as the BR112, but was quickly renamed N112; it became the N113 in 1988 when chassis changes were introduced.

Initial sales were slow, with Newport the only regular customer, but Scania has enjoyed considerably more success since the bus industry was deregulated and much of the public sector was privatised and lost its buy-British policy.

Scania K92

Built: Katrineholm, Sweden 1987.
Engine: Scania DS9.
Transmission: Scania automatic.
Bodywork: East Lancs.
Areas of operation: Maidstone, London.

The longitudinally-engined K92 (K93 from 1988) sells mainly as a coach in the UK, but a few have been imported as buses since 1985. These include four 11.2m East Lancs-bodied double-deckers supplied in 1987 to Maidstone Boro'line and Grey Green. All have CAG, a computer-controlled transmission based on a synchromesh gearbox. Air intakes to the nine-litre engine are on the nearside, behind the rear axle, and at the back.

Above:
Scania K92: Rear view of one of Grey-Green's two K92 double-deckers, showing the rear and nearside grilles on the **East Lancs** coach bodies.

BODYWORK
Alexander A, D, and J-types

Built: Falkirk, Stirlingshire.
Heights: High (A, J) and low (D).
Chassis: Leyland Atlantean, Daimler Fleetline, Dennis Dominator, MCW Metrobus.
Areas of operation: Central Scotland, Romford.

Alexander, now the world's biggest manufacturer of double-deck bus bodies, set a new trend in 1962 when its five-bay A-type body appeared with curved front windscreens from its Y-type single-decker. Over the years, the design evolved, gaining optional flat windscreens, peaked front and rear roof domes and panoramic windows (with every second window pillar omitted). On 10m chassis, they had an additional half-bay at the back. The 2.5m version is the J-type and lowheight vehicles, which have shallow windows on both decks, are designated D-type. From 1970, when alloy framing was introduced, they became AD and AJ.

The last D-types, mainly on Fleetlines for Scottish companies, were built in 1980, but five radically different versions were built in 1978/79 on Dominator and Metrobus chassis. They have top deck sections derived from the highbridge AL body, with peaked front and rear roof domes. Separate flat upper deck windscreens and squarer drivers' windscreens. The two Dominators (operated latterly by Kelvin Central and Maidstone & District) have five-bay bodies and deeper upper deck side windows giving a top-heavy look. The Metrobuses (with Kelvin Central and Capital Citybus) have four-bay bodies to match the MCW chassis frames and, being of a 13ft 10in intermediate height, have equal depth side windows.

Below:
Alexander AD: Shallow lower deck windows help identify the lowheight body on this Clydeside Fleetline. Earlier versions of this body had more elaborate lower front dash panels.

Above:
Alexander AD: One of three Metrobuses fitted with an unusual version of the AD body, with longer window bays and peaked roof domes. This one is in the Ensign (now Capital) Citybus fleet in Romford, but was new to Midland Scottish.

Alexander AL-type

Built: Falkirk, Stirlingshire.
Height: High.
Chassis: Leyland Atlantean, Daimler Fleetline, Bristol VRT.
Areas of operation: Aberdeen, Edinburgh, Glasgow, Newcastle, Liverpool, Sheffield, Preston, Bournemouth, Northampton, Cardiff, Isle of Man, Northern Ireland.

The AL-type, built from 1972 to 1982, was basically a five-bay successor to the J-type. It uses aluminium alloy construction (hence the A prefix), has equal depth windows on both decks and is slightly more box-like in shape. As on its predecessor, 10m models have an extra half-bay at the rear. Within the basic shape, there have been many variations — short bays and panoramic windows (sometimes together where weaker panoramic window bodies have later been rebuilt); curved or flat windscreens; rounded or peaked roof domes; engine fairings or full bustle. Merseyside, which bought AL bodies throughout its production life, specified a different side window arrangement with more pronounced pillars. Bristol VRTs were fitted with large front grilles; the front dash mouldings on Atlantean and Fleetlines varied over the years.

Above right:
Alexander AL: An OK Travel Atlantean, ex-Tyne & Wear PTE, with radiused roof domes, panoramic windows and vee-shaped windscreen.

Right:
Alexander AL: Front and rear views of peaked dome, short window versions on Portsmouth Atlanteans. This also shows the effect of curved windscreens.

Alexander AV-type

Built: Falkirk, Stirlingshire.
Heights: High and low.
Chassis: Volvo Ailsa.
Areas of operation: Central Scotland, Leeds.

Alexander bodied the two Ailsa prototypes and most of the buses sold in the model's first years. Until 1980, these were to the five-bay AV design similar to the AL, but always distinguishable by the lack of a rear engine and by their offside cab door, three-leaf passenger door and large upward-hinged radiator grille. Fifteen Strathclyde vehicles were built in 1975 with curved front and rear roof domes and curved upper deck windscreen (one has since been rebuilt as a single-decker), but all other AVs have peaked roof domes with separate, flat upper windscreens. Drivers' windscreens are curved on most bodies, but 53 West Midlands Ailsas (all sold and scattered among smaller operators) had flat vee-shaped screens. A lowheight prototype (operated latterly by Eagre Coaches of Gainsborough, Lincs) has the same top-heavy appearance of the AD-type Dominators of 1978.

Below:
Alexander AV: An ex-West Midlands Ailsa operated by Skill's of Nottingham. It has a vee-shaped windscreen and square upper deck windscreens to accommodate the opening vents at the top. The three-leaf entrance door is just visible through the nearside lower deck windscreen.

Above:
Alexander R: A highbridge R-type, with the vee screens, on a South Yorkshire Dennis Dominator, showing the squarer grille on earlier versions of this body.

Alexander R-type

Built: Falkirk, Stirlingshire; Mallusk, Co Antrim.
Heights: High and low.
Chassis: Dennis Dominator; Iveco TurboCity; Leyland Olympian, Lion; MCW Metrobus; Scania N113/N113; Volvo Citybus, Ailsa.
Areas of operation: London, Central Scotland, Aberdeen, Birmingham, Newcastle, Liverpool, Sheffield, West Yorkshire, Leicester, Nottingham, Hull, Newport, Oxford, Cardiff, Weston-super-Mare, Burnley, Northampton, Grimsby, Maidstone, Southend, Colchester, Swindon, Hampshire, Bedfordshire, Lancashire, Cumbria, Sussex.
The R-type, introduced in 1980, is a four-bay body (with extra centre half-bay on 10m bodies and five bays on three 12m Olympians for Stagecoach). In highbridge form it has deep, equal depth side windows on both decks; in lowheight form it has shallower, equal depth side windows. Both versions have the same deep upper deck windscreens with a pointed effect and a choice of either curved or flat glazing. Tayside has Citybuses with separately-mounted front glasses. On lowheights, the upper deck side windows stop before the bottom of the front windscreen and the lower deck side windows stop short of the doors and the top of the driver's windscreen. The driver's windscreen (deeper on some models) can either be flat vee-shaped, flat with quarter-lights, curved, or BET-style double-curvature. All

31

Above left:
Alexander R: A 10m lowheight body, with centre half-bay on an Olympian in the Stagecoach group's United Counties fleet. It has a later design of grille.

Left:
Alexander R: Another lowheight Olympian, but a 9.5m Olympian version with BET-style windscreen and curved lower dash. It is operated by City of Oxford.

Above:
Alexander RDC: One of the two highbridge coach-bodied Volvo Citybuses operated by Western Scottish. *Stewart J. Brown*

more recent models have small grilles (of different style on Strathclyde Citybuses), but Ailsas and early Citybuses have the large Ailsa grille from the AV body and earlier Scanias have a plain front. The Mallusk factory has built R-type Olympians for export to Dublin Bus.

Four 11m five-bay coach derivatives, type RDC, went to SBG companies in 1984. Two lowheight Olympians are operated by SMT, two highbridge Citybuses by Western. They have square cornered bonded glazing, a largely glazed front end, a sloping back and a single-piece coach door. The Olympians give the illusion of being longer than the Volvos.

East Lancs

Built: Blackburn, Lancashire.
Height: High and low.
Chassis: Leyland Atlantean, Olympian; Daimler Fleetline; Bristol VRT; Dennis Dominator; Volvo Ailsa, Citybus; Scania N112, N113, K92.
Areas of operation: London, Dundee, Blackburn, Blackpool, Brighton, Cardiff, Derby, Eastbourne, Ipswich, Leicester, Lincoln, Maidstone, Plymouth, Preston, Southampton, Warrington, Liverpool, Manchester, Swindon, Sheffield, Newport, Bournemouth, Great Yarmouth, Northampton.

The standard five-bay East Lancs body has been in production on rear-engined buses since the early 1960s and has been updated gradually and offered with several permutations of front windscreens which can radically alter its appearance. East Lancs, now owned by Drawlane Transport and principal bodybuilder to its operating subsidiaries, is probably the last builder of bespoke buses for the British market.

In its most common form, the five-bay body is relatively square with equal depth windows on both decks. At 10m, it has longer rather than extra bays. The upper deck front windscreens are raked back slightly and many may have large upper deck emergency door windows and lower deck rear windows. This latter feature, most common on Atlanteans and Fleetlines, is to help drivers when reversing. Front roof domes can be flat, peaked or rounded; upper deck windscreens are either separate flat glasses, flat vertically-divided glasses, one piece flat or one-piece or divided double-curvature; and drivers' windscreens are either one-piece flat, divided flat, or curved in Alexander style (one-piece or divided). Side windows are usually gasket glazed with either round or square corners, but some have bonded glazing. More recently, four-bay bodies have been built, usually with double-curvature windscreens; some of these are lowheight Olympians and Dominators for Drawlane companies.

Since 1984, East Lancs has also built bodies which closely resemble the Alexander R-type. The first 18, Dominators for South Yorkshire Transport and Leicester Citybus, are barely distinguishable from SYT's R-types; they have a ventilation louvre on the staircase panel, in line with the bottom of the lower deck windows, and the lower deck emergency

---

Below:
East Lancs: A five-bay body, with flat windscreens and separate upper deck windscreens, on a Merseybus Atlantean. It also has the unique style of window mountings specified for most of the operator's double-deckers in the 1970s. The bus alongside is a **Metrobus Mk 2** with flat windscreen.

door window stops short of the tops of the main bay windows. Scanias, Volvos and Dominators for Hull, Grimsby, Newport and Grey-Green have standard East Lancs large upper deck emergency doors and an additional moulding strap between the two decks, a few inches above the lower deck windows. Just to add to the variety, Hull has Scanias with five-bay windows and Alexander-style fronts.

Above:
East Lancs: A four-bay body, with sloping roof dome and curved windscreens, on a Nottingham Scania N113. The bus was previously operated by A1 Service in Ayrshire.

Below:
East Lancs: One of the unusual Kingston upon Hull Scania N113s with Alexander-style fronts on five-bay bodies. The side panelling arrangement, with a horizontal panel join running a few inches above the lower deck windows, also helps identify the four-bay Alexander-style bodies.

ECW (see Leyland)

Leyland (including ECW, Park Royal, Roe)

A series of acquisitions and mergers led to Leyland owning Eastern Coach Works, Park Royal and Roe. It closed Park Royal in 1980, Roe in 1984 and ECW in 1987. Optare, which re-opened the Roe works in 1985, built a few bodies under contract, but the ECW jigs were transferred to Leyland's Workington plant and production resumed there from 1988 to 1991.

ECW 1966-81 standard

Built: Lowestoft, Suffolk.
Heights: High and low.
Chassis: Bristol VRT, Daimler Fleetline, Leyland Atlantean.
Areas of operation: Throughout Britain.

When Bristol developed the VRT, ECW simply adapted the basic design of five-bay body used on the front-engined Lodekka FLF of 1960 for the new chassis and for the Fleetline and Atlantean. This has equal depth windows on both decks, narrow window pillars, separately mounted upper deck front windscreens and (on 9.5m chassis) a short upper deck side window above the engine. On highbridge bodies, the lower deck windows are higher than the driver's side window.

All bodies built until 1972, when the Series 2 VRT was introduced, had flat windscreens; most built afterwards (including all Series 2 and 3 VRTs) had BET-style double-curvature windscreens. Sixty-two 1975 Atlanteans and Fleetlines for Colchester and South Yorkshire had peaked front and rear roof domes, vee-shaped flat drivers' windscreens with quarterlights.

Below:
ECW: The standard lowheight ECW body on an Eastern National (Badgerline group) Bristol VRT Series 3. Note the engine cooling vent below the rearmost side window.

Above:
ECW: Highbridge version of the standard body, on a Trent Atlantean. The lower deck windows are set higher and there is more space between the decks at the front.

Below:
Roe: One of the last BET-style bodies on an Atlantean in Hull's Citilink fleet.

Roe BET-style

Built: Leeds, West Yorkshire.
Height: High.
Chassis: Leyland Atlantean.
Area of operation: Hull, Leeds.

Roe built a steel-framed body in the 1960s, mainly for some of the old BET group companies. These are similar to contemporary MCW bodies, with shallow upper deck windows, curved front and rear domes and relatively flat sides. The last significant fleet, refurbished by Kingston upon Hull City Transport shortly before deregulation, have an unusual design of sloping flat windscreen. Yorkshire Rider has some ex-Leeds Atlanteans with bodies derived from this design, but with peaked roof domes and panoramic side windows.

Park Royal/Roe 1968-81

Built: Park Royal, West London; Leeds, West Yorkshire.
Height: High.
Chassis: Daimler Fleetline, Leyland Atlantean.
Areas of operation: London, Brighton, Manchester, Birmingham, Leeds, Nottingham, Derby, Lancashire, Liverpool.

Park Royal and Roe developed this square profile four-bay body with equal depth windows on both decks and sides which taper in from the base of the upper windows. It is built on 9.5m and 10m chassis, the more common 9.5m having a short bay above the engine compartment. For a time, this was the standard body for London Transport, West and South Yorkshire, Greater Manchester and West Midlands PTEs and for some NBC companies.

Below:
Park Royal: The Alexander-style windscreen and three-piece lower dash on this ex-Plymouth Atlantean in the Ensign Citybus fleet are features most common on similar buses supplied to NBC fleets. The round roof dome was standard, but West Yorkshire PTE had peaked domes and London Transport specified square domes, barrel windscreens and plain lower dash.

Both bodybuilders made them with either curved or peaked front roof domes, but for the Yorkshire PTEs, Roe built them with a more rounded peaked dome. The standard driver's windscreen was vee-shaped with flat glass, but buses for NBC, Plymouth and Nottingham had Alexander-style two-piece curved windscreens and more elaborate lower front panels, while London Transport specified barrel-shaped windscreens. Compared with similar MCW bodies, the Park Royal/Roe products have a single-piece front and rear roof dome and lower deck emergency doors which stop flush with the tops of the side windows.

Olympian body

Built: Lowestoft, Suffolk; Leeds, West Yorkshire; Workington, Cumbria.
Heights: High and low.
Chassis: Leyland Olympian, Atlantean.
Areas of operation: Throughout Britain (notably London, Glasgow, Edinburgh, Newcastle, Liverpool, Manchester, Birmingham, Bristol, Preston, Isle of Man, Isle of Wight, Derby, Nottingham, Leicester, Colchester, Reading, Cambridge, Norwich, Oxford).
The four-bay Leyland body for the Olympians was developed from the Titan body, but has shallower lower deck windows. In lowheight form, the windows on both decks are of equal depth. The rear upper deck emergency door on most has much more glazing than on the London Titans. In standard 9.5m form, it has equal length bays, but 10m bodies, including one built on an Atlantean with Fishwick's of Leyland, have a shorter bay in the middle, as on London's RML Routemasters.

ECW and Roe built highbridge bodies with flat, vee-shaped two-piece drivers' windscreens and with Alexander-shaped two-piece double-curvature screens; ECW built high and low models with BET-style windscreens. Optare has built highbridge bodies with vee-

Below:
Roe Olympian: Strapping over the panel joins identifies the highbridge Roe body on this Cambus Olympian, one of several sold by West Yorkshire PTE in 1986 when newly-formed Yorkshire Rider declined to take on the leases on some of the recent buses. This bus has a vee-shaped windscreen, but Roe also built them with Alexander-style windscreens like those on the Ensign Atlantean.

screens and BET screens and Workington built high and low models with BET screens. A key identification point is that Roe bodies and the first 15 Optare bodies (1985 vehicles operated now by Yorkshire Rider) have strapping over the panel joins on the sides.

ECW produced coach versions, mostly for 11m chassis, from 1982. Early models have large, flat upper-deck windscreens raked back sharply and BET drivers' windscreens; later vehicles have more upright double-curvature upper deck windscreens and single-curvature drivers' windscreens. South Yorkshire Transport bought a 1984 prototype to the newer style and with bonded glazing.

Below:
ECW Olympian: A London Buses highbridge Olympian with one of the last ECW bodies built. Similar bodies are built at Workington.

Right:
ECW Olympian: One of the first style of 11m coaches with the odd mix of BET driver's windscreen and raked, flat upper windscreen.

Below right:
ECW Olympian: An 11m example of the later style of coach, with curved upper deck windscreen, in service with Eastern National on a London commuter service.

Marshall

Built: Cambridge.
Height: High.
Chassis: Dennis Dominator; Leyland Atlantean, Olympian; Scania N112; Volvo Ailsa, City-bus.
Areas of operation: Glasgow, Merseyside, Leicester, South Yorkshire, Newport, Derby.
Marshall started building double-deck bodies in 1978, on two Leicester Dominators. The four-bay design tapers in quite starkly from the base of the upper deck windows. The Leicester vehicles have equal depth windows on both decks, but most have deeper lower deck windows. Upper deck windscreens are either two separate flat glasses or vee-shaped; on most vehicles, there is a heavily-lidded dome, but later Derby Citybuses have taller windscreens which create a pointed effect. Drivers' windscreens are either vee-shaped flat or BET-style double-curvature.

Below:
Marshall: The heavily peaked front roof dome and deep lower deck windows are apparent on one of 30 Marshall-bodied Atlanteans operated by South Yorkshire.

Metro-Cammell Weymann

Built: Birmingham.
Height: High.
Chassis: Bristol VRT, Daimler Fleetline, Leyland Atlantean.
Areas of operation: Newcastle, London, Birmingham.
MCW's last body as an independent supplier, available from 1969 to 1979, is very similar to the Park Royal/Roe product of the same period, but differs by having a taller lower deck emergency exit, moulding lines around the front and rear roof domes at window top height and a smaller glazed area on the upper deck emergency door. Most had flat, vee-shaped drivers' windscreens, but those built for London and South Yorkshire had barrel-shaped windscreens.

Top:
MCW: An ex-West Midlands Fleetline, with shallow windscreen and operator-specified destination display, operated by Amberley in Leeds.

Above:
MCW: The emergency doors, with small window on the top deck and tall door and prominent guttering on the lower deck, help identify the MCW body on one of London Buses' DMS-class Fleetlines.

Northern Counties

Built: Wigan, Greater Manchester.
Heights: High and low.
Chassis: Daimler Fleetline; Dennis Dominator; Leyland Atlantean, Olympian; MCW Metrobus; Scania N112, N113; Volvo Ailsa, Citybus.
Areas of operation: Manchester, London, Teesside, Glasgow, West Yorkshire, Newcastle, Liverpool, Maidstone, Canterbury, Norwich, Cambridge, Peterborough, Isle of Man, Hull, Preston, Sheffield, Fife.

Northern Counties' four-bay body developed out of the needs of SELNEC (later Greater Manchester) PTE, which became a major shareholder in the business. It bears a strong superficial resemblance to the Park Royal/Roe and MCW designs, but there are notable differences. It has thicker pillars to the sides of the upper deck front windscreens; a longer half-bay at the back of the upper deck of 9.5m models; a larger upper deck emergency door window; and most have ventilation louvres at the centre of the front roof dome. Earlier buses have flat, vee-shaped drivers' windscreens, but most have curved or barrel-shaped

---

Below:
Northern Counties: The destination screens, with large number and intermediate point displays, help identify these Fareway of Liverpool Fleetlines as ex-Greater Manchester buses. They have the early style of Northern Counties standard body, with flat windscreens on both decks and grille on the front roof dome. They are passing a Merseybus Atlantean with **Alexander AL** body.

Right:
Northern Counties: One of 10 Dominators in the South Yorkshire fleet with Alexander driver's windscreen, lower dash and pillar spacing.   *Adrian Thomas*

Below right:
Northern Counties: A later version of the standard body for Greater Manchester. This Metrobus has separately-mounted upper deck windscreens and a thicker pillar behind the first upper deck window.

Above:
Northern Counties: The latest version of the standard body, with peaked front roof dome and wider grille, on a Capital Citybus Dennis Dominator. The bus on the left is an older Fylde Borough Atlantean refurbished with the new-style front end and a false grille.

---

ones. Newer vehicles have recessed windows and separately-mounted upper deck front windscreens. Ten South Yorkshire Dominators have Alexander R-type pillar spacing, drivers' windscreens and lower front dash within the basic Northern Counties shape.

From 1988, the design was modified to gain peaked front roof domes, restyled upper deck emergency door and a new lower front dash with a wide, shallow grille. Pillar spacings on these and the earlier bodies differ according to the length of chassis. On 9.5m chassis, there is a small window between the entrance door and the front wheel and there is a thicker pillar after the first top deck side windows; longer vehicles lack these features, but on the new body, 9.8m Olympians have a short window immediately ahead of the engine compartment. From 1992, this body has been named the Countybus Palatine.

Park Royal/Roe (see Leyland)

Willowbrook

Built: Loughborough, Leicestershire.
Height: High.
Chassis: Bristol VRT, Leyland Atlantean, Dennis Dominator.
Areas of operation: Melton Mowbray, Liverpool, Canterbury.
Willowbrook developed a body used on front-engined chassis when it first bodied rear-engined double-deckers. It has heavy-looking front and rear domes with three drainage gutters on the front dome, flat windscreens on both decks, those on the upper deck being mounted separately within thick pillars.

From 1977 to 1981, 117 bodies were built to a four-bay design similar to the Park Royal/Roe/MCW standard, but with a much more upright rear end and with BET-style double-curvature drivers' windscreens.

Above:
Willowbrook: One of the last examples of the old Willowbrook double-deck bodies on a rebodied ex-Trent Atlantean in the Barton fleet.   *Roy Marshall*

Below:
Willowbrook: The square quasi-Park Royal/Roe/MCW body on an East Kent Bristol VRT. The lower dash is similar to that on ECW VRTs.

Nottingham East Lancs: Single-width entrance door, heavy front bumper, shallow roof dome and a mix of bonded and gasket glazing are some of the highly individual features of this Nottingham Atlantean with East Lancs body.

Nottingham City Transport

Bodybuilders: East Lancs, Northern Counties, Willowbrook.
Height: High.
Chassis: Leyland Atlantean, Olympian, Lion; Volvo Citybus; Daimler Fleetline.

Alone among British bus operators, Nottingham persisted in laying down its own specification for double-deckers until 1988. It evolved from the mid-1960s (when MCW also built it) and was retained to reduce the number of body parts held in stock, to provide maximum body strength and seating capacity on both decks. Latterly, single-width entrance doors were specified. It uses short window bays and a shallow front dome with double-curvature upper deck windscreen and BET-style driver's windscreen. The lower deck rear window is tall to give maximum reversing visibility and the destination screen is set at a downward angle immediately above the driver's windscreen. Some former Nottingham buses, many converted to open-top, are operated in historic towns and cities (eg Stratford, Oxford, Cambridge, Edinburgh) by Guide Friday. Nottingham's two Northern Counties-bodied Olympians are owned by Buffalo Travel in Bedfordshire. Darlington has some Fleetlines.

Below:
Nottingham Northern Counties: Amidst all the Nottingham features, this Atlantean has the style of small rear upper deck emergency door fitted by Northern Counties until the 1970s. The large rear lower deck window, a Nottingham requirement, was standard on all East Lancs bodies built at the time.

PART 2 SINGLE-DECK BUSES

Chassis identification of single-deckers is more difficult than for double-deckers as the bodybuilder is better able to disguise chassis features, especially on mid and front-engined vehicles. Because of this, the emphasis on those two areas is in identifying bodywork.

CHASSIS AND INTEGRALS — REAR-ENGINED

ACE Cougar

Built: Huddersfield, West Yorkshire 1990 to date.
Engine: Perkins Phaser.
Transmission: Allison automatic.
Bodywork: Wadham Stringer, Willowbrook.
Areas of operation: Portsmouth, Solihull.

Alternative Chassis Engineering was formed in 1984 after the Ward company went into receivership. After a period of inactivity, it launched the 10.5m Cougar in 1990 into the growing single-deck market. It has air suspension. Only three had been built by the end of 1991.

Below:
ACE Cougar: The first Cougar, with **Wadham Stringer Portsdown** body, has been bought by People's Provincial to assess its suitability as a replacement for its large fleet of Leyland Nationals.

AEC Swift

Built: Southall, Middlesex 1964-74.
Engine: (principal survivors) AEC AH505.
Transmission: AEC semi-automatic.
Bodywork: (principal survivors) ECW, Willowbrook.
Area of operation: Great Yarmouth.

The Swift was one of the more commercially successful, but nonetheless mechanically troublesome first generation of low-floor rear-engined urban single-deckers. At one time, London Transport had 1,500. The engine is mounted horizontally behind the rear axle and the radiator is to the offside of the engine compartment.

Above:
AEC Swift: Great Yarmouth is the last operator to have run Swifts since new. This one has an **ECW** body of a style more common on Bristol REs, but identifiable by the plain front dash and grille at the rear.

Bristol RE

Built: Bristol 1962-82.
Engines: Gardner 6HLX, Leyland 680.
Transmission: Self-Changing Gears semi-automatic.
Bodywork: ECW, Alexander, East Lancs, Marshall.
Areas of operation: Northern Ireland, Tyneside, Teesside, Hartlepool, Greater Manchester, Bexhill, Wells, Milton Keynes, Sheffield.

The RE not only sold well, but enjoyed the best reputation of the first generation rear-engined single-deckers. It was kept in production longest for Ulsterbus and Citybus in Northern Ireland which insisted on buying a relatively simple Gardner-engined chassis which could be bodied locally by Alexander. It was the standard single-decker for many NBC companies before the arrival of the Leyland National. It has a horizontal engine and front radiator. Bus versions were the 10m RESL and 11m RELL; higher floor coaches were the 10m RESH, 11m RELH and 12m REMH. ECW bodies on 11m REs have six main window bays; 10m models have five. These are equal depth side windows with slim window pillars. From 1967, they had flat fronts with shallow, vertically-divided windscreens; from 1969 the windscreen was taller; and from 1970 it was to BET curved style. Bus versions have a centrally-mounted emergency door at the back, flanked by two tall windows; RELH semi-coaches have a large rear window and offside emergency door.

Above:
Bristol RE: An **ECW**-bodied RELL, new to Crosville, but operating in Stockton on Tees with a small operator. Note the front grille and BET-style windscreen.

Daimler Fleetline SRG

Built: Coventry 1966-74.
Engines: Gardner 6LX.
Transmission: Self-Changing Gears semi-automatic.
Bodywork: (principal survivors) Roe.
Area of operation: Darlington.

Daimler built 334 10m and 11m single-deck versions of the Fleetline, 24 for Darlington, whose last examples were still running in 1991. The engine compartment is boxed in and has a three-piece cover with lifting centre section and outward opening sides.

Below:
Daimler Fleetline SRG: One of Darlington's 11m single-deck Fleetlines with **Roe** bodywork.

Dennis Falcon

Built: Guildford, Surrey 1980 to date.
Engines: Gardner 6HLXB, 6HLXCT.
Transmission: Voith, SCG, Maxwell automatic.
Bodywork: Duple, East Lancs, Marshall, Wadham Stringer, Northern Counties.
Areas of operation: Grimsby, Hartlepool, Accrington, Ipswich, Swindon, Merseyside, Staffordshire.

After selling single-deck versions of the Dominator, Dennis developed the Falcon to fill the void left when Leyland withdrew the Gardner-engined Bristol RE from the market. There are two versions, the Falcon H with remote located gearbox and the more common HC with gearbox coupled to the engine to give a shorter rear overhang. Both sold mainly to municipal operators, but the HC model sold more recently to Drawlane companies North Western and Midland Red North.

Below:
Dennis Falcon H: An Ipswich Falcon with a flat-sided **East Lancs** body. It has a stepped-down side window arrangement and an off-centre front grille.

Dennis Domino

Built: Guildford, Surrey 1985.
Engine: Perkins T6.354.4.
Transmission: Maxwell automatic.
Bodywork: Northern Counties, Optare.
Areas of operation: Manchester, Stockport.

The 7.8m Domino, in essence a scaled-down Dominator, is a transverse rear-engined midibus developed for intensive urban work. It has a turbocharged engine, front radiator, full air suspension and power steering. Only 34 were built, for Greater Manchester and South Yorkshire; most of the 14 South Yorkshire vehicles were sold to Stevensons of Uttoxeter for use in Stockport and south Manchester and the West Midlands.

Above:
Dennis Domino: A Greater Manchester Buses Domino with **Northern Counties** body on the Manchester Centreline service.

Below:
Dennis Dart: Rear view of a **Wadham Stringer**-bodied 9m Dart showing the offside grille and rear engine access.

Dennis Dart

Built: Guildford, Surrey 1988 to date.
Engine: Cummins 6BT.
Transmission: Allison automatic.
Bodywork: Carlyle, Duple, Wadham Stringer, Wright, Reeve Burgess, East Lancs, Alexander, Northern Counties.
Areas of operation: London, Tyneside, Warrington, Greater Manchester, Barnsley, Eastbourne, Southampton, Walsall, Watford, Kent, Chester, Staffordshire, Sussex, Glasgow, Inverness, Anglesey, York.

Dennis replaced the Domino with the Dart, a far more successful vehicle which had won over 700 orders by 1992. It has been bought by several divisions of London Buses, by the Stagecoach group and Go-Ahead Northern, among others. It has a longitudinal vertical engine with offside radiator and has leaf suspension. The Dart is built in three lengths, 8.5m, 9m and 9.8m, offering maximum seating capacities of 35 to 43 passengers.

Dennis Lance

Built: Guildford, Surrey 1991 to date.
Engine: Cummins 6CTA.
Transmission: ZF automatic.
Bodywork: Alexander, East Lancs, Plaxton, Wadham Stringer.
Areas of operation: Ipswich, London, Eastbourne.

Building on the success of the Dart, Dennis has introduced the 10.5m and 11.5m Lance to compete in the citybus market. It has a longitudinal vertical engine, offside radiator in the engine compartment and air suspension. Unlike the Falcon, which has a ramped floor, the Lance floor is flat to the rear axle.

Below:
Dennis Lance: The engine installation of the Lance is apparent in this rear view of one with **Plaxton Verde** body.

Ikarus Citibus

Built: Budapest, Hungary and Eindhoven, Netherlands 1990 to date.
Chassis: DAF SB220.
Engine: DAF 11.6-litre.
Transmission: ZF automatic.
Areas of operation: Tyneside, West Yorkshire, Maidstone, Birmingham, London.

Ikarus, as well as being one of Hungary's largest industrial concerns, was the former Soviet Bloc's main bus manufacturer and is generally reckoned to be the world's largest supplier of buses and coaches. It was trying to diversify into western markets before the Soviet system collapsed and developed the 400-Series of steel-framed citybuses for American and other markets. In Britain, it is fitted on horizontal-engined DAF SB220 chassis more commonly found as the basis of the Optare Delta and is imported through Hughes DAF, the DAF Bus distributor. Its most distinguishing features are its large curved windscreen with wiper mountings which create the illusion of a downswept windscreen and Hungarian black-on-white route number blinds. It has a wide entrance and ramped floor. They are available with two doors, vertically divided windscreens and electronic destination displays.

Below:
Ikarus Citibus: The windscreen wipers on this Maidstone Boro'line Ikarus-bodied DAF SB220 create the illusion of a sloping windscreen. Note the Hungarian route number blinds.

Leyland National and B21

Built: Workington, Cumbria 1971-85.
Engines: Leyland 510, 680, 690, TL11H; Gardner 6HLXB, 6HLXCT; Volvo THD100; DAF 11.6-litre.
Transmission: Leyland semi- and fully-automatic; ZF automatic.
Areas of operation: Throughout Britain, Isle of Man.

By far the most numerous of all rear-engined single-deckers is the Leyland National, of which over 7,000 were built. It is an integral construction, highly standardised design built using mass production lessons learned after Leyland bought the Standard-Triumph and Rover car companies in the 1960s. Leyland's Workington factory was designed for National production in a joint venture with NBC (hence the name), which was the biggest customer. Nationals were also bought by all seven conurbation PTEs, by London Transport, most

Above:
Leyland National: A 10.3m Mk 1 National, with roof pod, in the Sovereign fleet at Stevenage. Note the longer window ahead of the rear axle.

Right:
Leyland National 2: An 11.6m National 2, without roof pod, in Yorkshire Traction's Mexborough & Swinton livery.

Below right:
Leyland National Greenway: The original National body lines are still identifiable behind the flat vee-windscreen and lower dash of the first East Lancs rebuild, a National 2 for London & Country.

SBG companies, many municipals, a handful of independents and major airports. They have proved popular secondhand buys for many new operators of local bus services since deregulation in 1986. The body shell was also used for some of British Rail's Pacer railcar fleet.

They have equal depth windows along the length of the body, a two-piece double-curvature windscreen and an angled roofline. Destination screens are to a common design and there is provision for a display above the large rear window.

Mk 1 models, built until 1979, had Leyland 510 engines and rear-mounted radiators with a grille on the back end. Until 1978, when the simpler Series B option was introduced, all Mk 1 models had a heating pod mounted at the rear of the roof (from 1976 this became shorter); Series B models have floor-mounted heaters, no roof pod and a small grille between the headlamps. The Mk 2, which appeared in prototype form in 1978 looking like a Series B, went into production in 1979 with the 680 engine in place of the ill-received 510, a front-mounted radiator and a more bulbous windscreen. Roof pods and plain roofs were available for this model which later was offered with Gardner engines and the quieter TL11H which ultimately ousted the 680.

Two lengths were built throughout the National's life. On Mk 1 models, these were 10.3m or 11.3m; in Mk 2 form, they were 10.6m and 11.6m to accommodate the front radiator. Long models have equal length windows in the main bays; short models have a longer bay immediately ahead of the rear axle, where a centre door can be fitted.

Many Nationals, especially Mk 1s, have been re-powered with Gardner, Leyland 680, Volvo and DAF engines and some have had their bodies refurbished. In 1991, East Lancs launched a refurbishment package called the National Greenway designed to add 10 years' life to ageing Nationals. New fronts, with flat vee-shaped windscreens and quarterlights, flat

59

lower dash panels, curved rear ends from the EL2000 body, two-leaf doors, lower entrance steps and remounted side windows with square top corners are the most noticeable changes which also involve a complete interior refit.

For export markets which insisted on buying locally-bodied chassis, Leyland developed the semi-integral B21 underframe in 1975 with National running gear and front radiator. It was built at Bristol. Ulsterbus and Citybus bought six with Alexander (Belfast) bodies and Leyland and Gardner engines in 1980, when RE production was ending, and Ipswich had four Bristol-badged Leyland-engined 12m models, cancelled by an export customer, bodied by Alexander (Belfast) in 1984. Ipswich has since bought the Ulster vehicles.

Leyland Lynx

Built: Workington, Cumbria 1985-91.
Engines: Cummins L10, Volvo THD102, Leyland TL11H, Gardner 6HLXC.
Transmission: ZF or Leyland automatic.
Bodywork: Leyland, Alexander.
Areas of operation: Throughout UK (notably London, Edinburgh, West Midlands, Preston, Colchester, Maidstone, West Yorkshire, Teesside, Bristol. Nottingham, Newcastle, Widnes, Wrexham, Essex, Isle of Man, Cardiff.
In place of the National, Leyland developed an 11.3m semi-integral underframe with a simpler driveline from the horizontal rear engine to the gearbox. It has a front radiator. The standard Workington body has flat sides, deep side windows with bonded glazing, squared-off wheel arches, an arched roofline and flat windscreens, the driver's half of which is angled back in the fashion of British buses of the 1950s. Mk 1 versions have flat fronts and a split step entrance; Mk 2 models, introduced in 1990, have a protruding grille and lower dash panel to accommodate intercoolers on Volvo-engined buses, and a level entrance step. Six of the first Lynxes were supplied to Ulsterbus and Citybus in 1985 with Alexander (Belfast) bodies, but have been sold to Stevensons of Uttoxeter. The Lynx is being replaced by Volvo's new B10B rear-engined chassis.

Below:
Leyland Lynx: The flatter front end and split-level entrance of the original Lynx, here operated by Millers of Cambridge.

Above:
Leyland Lynx II: The bulbous front of the Lynx II is to accommodate an intercooler in front of the radiator on Volvo-engined buses like this one for Nottingham. *Volvo Bus*

Mercedes-Benz O.405

Built: Mannheim, Germany (for UK) 1992 to date:
Engine: Mercedes OM447h
Transmission: ZF or Voith automatic.
Bodywork: Alexander.
Area of operation: Aberdeen.
The 11.5m O.405 has been produced for the German market since 1984 and has a horizontal rear engine, offside radiator in the engine compartment and air suspension. Mercedes hopes to build on its success in the UK minibus market by selling chassis and front ends with Alexander PS-type bodies. The first, an O.405G articulated bus, is being bought by Grampian Transport.

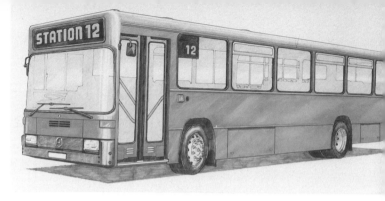

Mercedes-Benz O.405: An artist's impression of how the Mercedes front end will be grafted on to the **Alexander PS** body. *W. Alexander & Co*

Neoplan N416 SLII

Built: Stuttgart, Germany (for UK) 1987.
Engine: Gardner 6HLXCT.
Transmission: ZF automatic.
Area of operation: Sheffield.
Neoplan, better known in the UK as an importer of exotic luxury coaches, sold two city-buses to SUT, a company then in common ownership with Carlton PSV, the Neoplan importer. Plans to sell another 13 in the UK came to nought and SUT became part of South Yorkshire Transport. SLII is the designation applied to standard Neoplan, Setra, Mercedes-Benz and MAN citybuses for the VöV group of West German municipal operators. The UK vehicles are a simpler one-door version with Gardner engine; they have bonded glazing.

Neoplan N416: One of the two Neoplan SLII-type single-deckers bought by SUT and subsequently operated in South Yorkshire's Sheaf Line fleet. *Stewart J. Brown*

Optare Delta

Built: Leeds, West Yorkshire and Eindhoven, Netherlands 1988 to date.
Chassis: DAF SB220.
Engine: DAF: 11.6-litre.
Transmission: ZF automatic.
Areas of operation: London, Gatwick and Stansted airports, Birmingham, Manchester, North Wales, Tyneside, Teesside, Durham, Blackpool, Edinburgh, Derby, Nottingham, Canterbury, Staffordshire, Leeds, Ipswich.

The first full-size bus developed by Optare, following its stylish mini and midibuses, the 11.8m Delta is also the first British version of the DAF SB220 citybus. It is built using the Alusuisse bolted aluminium system and has a flat floor with steps to the rear section. The most distinctive feature is the large curved windscreen, with quarterlights, and front overhang to accommodate the front radiator.

Below:
Optare Delta: Ralph's Coaches operates two-door Deltas on the long-term car park shuttle service at Stansted Airport.

Optare Vecta

Built: Leeds, West Yorkshire and Salzgitter, Germany 1991 to date.
Chassis: MAN 11.180.
Engine: MAN DO826 TOH.
Transmission: ZF automatic.
Area of operation: Teesside, Campbeltown.

The Vecta, a 10.1m scaled down version of the Delta, is based on a MAN chassis more common in the UK market as the basis of a small coach. It has a low emission vertical rear engine, mounted longitudinally, and air suspension. As its radiator is mounted in the nearside of the engine compartment, it has a shorter front overhang than the Delta; the windscreen is single-piece and more upright. The first two Vectas were bought by Teesside Motor Services, a third by West Coast Motors.

Above:
Optare Vecta: As well as having fewer side windows, the Vecta has a more upright single-piece windscreen and a grille at the rear.

Renault PR100

Built: Lyons, France (for UK) 1988/89.
Engine: Renault MIPS 06.20.45.
Transmission: ZF automatic.
Bodywork: Northern Counties.
Areas of operation: Scunthorpe, Luton Airport, east London.
The PR100 was launched in the 1970s by Berliet, before Renault acquired the business from Peugeot/Citroen. Only five have been sold in the UK in a joint venture with Northern Counties, which built a steel-framed body between Renault-designed front and rear ends. The flat, sloping windscreen and deep quarterlights are its most distinguishing feature. Of the five buses, Luton Airport uses three on tarmac duties, one is operated by London Buses' East London company and the other was originally a demonstrator.

Below:
Renault PR100: Hornsby of Scunthorpe bought this former demonstration model from **Northern Counties.** Note the flat windscreen and deep quarterlights.   *Tim Carter*

Volvo B6R

Built: Vienna, Austria; Irvine, Ayrshire from 1992.
Engine: Volvo TD63E.
Transmission: Allison or ZF automatic.
Bodywork: Alexander, Reeve Burgess, Wright.
The B6R, developed by Volvo and Steyr, is a competitor for the Dennis Dart. It is available in 8.5m, 9m and 9.9m lengths, has air suspension, a longitudinal vertical engine and nearside radiator. First customers are the Stagecoach group, which has ordered 200 with Alexander bodies, with an option on 100 more, South Yorkshire Transport, taking one with Reeve Burgess body, with an option on 19 more and Stevensons taking two with Wright bodies.

Ward Dalesman GRXI

Built: Huddersfield, West Yorkshire 1983.
Engine: Gardner 6HLXB.
Transmission: Self-Changing Gears semi-automatic.
Bodywork: Wadham Stringer.
Area of operation: Darlington.
Darlington Transport bought six of the last Gardner-engined Seddon Pennine RUs in 1973 and, after a less happy experience with single-deck Dennis Dominators, persuaded Ward Motors to build an updated version of the RU. Six were supplied in 1983, but options on others could not be taken up as Ward went into receivership the following year. The GRXI — the designation stands for Gardner Rear IIm (Roman numerals) — has the same offside radiator position as the RU, ahead of the rear axle.

Below:
Ward Dalesman GRXI: One of Darlington's Wards with the original style of **Wadham Stringer Vanguard** body. The grille ahead of the rear axle is a feature carried forward from Darlington's Seddon RUs.

CHASSIS AND INTEGRALS — MID-ENGINED

AEC Reliance

Built: Southall, Middlesex 1953-79.
Engines: AEC AH470, AH505, AH590, AH691, AH760.
Transmission: AEC semi-automatic and synchromesh; ZF synchromesh.
Bodywork: Alexander, Duple, Marshall, Plaxton, Willowbrook.
The Reliance was one of the longest-lived underfloor-engined heavy-duty single-deckers on the market, graduating from a 30ft into a 12m vehicle which, latterly, was more popular as a coach than a bus. It ceased to be built when AEC's factory closed.

Bedford Y-Series/Venturer

Built: Dunstable, Bedfordshire 1970-86.
Engine: Bedford 8.3-litre.
Transmission: Spicer Turner, ZF synchromesh; Allison automatic.
Bodywork: Alexander, Duple, Marshall, Plaxton, Wadham Stringer, Wright, Willowbrook.
The lightweight Bedford range gained the underfloor-engined Y-Series from 1970. The vertical engine demanded a higher floor and ground clearance than horizontal engined chassis. It was once more common in larger fleets and is still popular with smaller independent companies. The YRQ, YLQ, YMQ and YMP are 10m models; YRT, YMT and YNT are 11m, YNV (Venturer) is 12m. YMQ/S conversions are shortened chassis for midibus work. Production ceased when General Motors closed Bedford's truck business.

Below:
Bristol LH: Contrast the fronts on these two **ECW**-bodied LHs in service in Stockton on Tees. The ex-London bus on the left is a narrow version with sidelights above the headlamps. The wider ex-Bristol Omnibus vehicle has the sidelights on the outside.

Bristol LH

Built: Bristol 1967-81.
Engines: Leyland 400, 401; Perkins H6/354.
Transmission: Turner synchromesh, Self-Changing Gears semi-automatic.
Bodywork: ECW, Alexander, Duple, East Lancs, Marshall, Plaxton, Wadham Stringer.
The horizontal-engined LH was developed as a 9.2m lightweight single-decker for NBC companies and, as such, was operated in many parts of England and Wales with ECW bodies. London Transport bought around 100 in the mid-1970s for routes which needed short, narrow buses. The 7.3m and 8.1m LHS remained in production longest; the 11m LHL was discontinued early in the model's history. The LH has a front radiator. ECW bodies on LHs have five main bays, a large single rear window and most have BET-style windscreens; the earliest had flat, vertically-divided windscreens. Wide and narrow bodies are most readily identified by the position of the front trafficator lights.

Dennis Dorchester

Built: Guildford, Surrey 1982-88.
Engines: Gardner 6HLXB, 6HLXCT.
Transmission: Voith automatic; Self-Changing Gears semi-automatic; ZF synchromesh.
Bodywork: Alexander, Reeve Burgess, Wadham Stringer.
Dennis built the heavy-duty Dorchester to satisfy a small demand for Gardner-engined single-deckers. Most common as a coach, it sold as a bus to Central Scottish, Tillingbourne Bus and to Geoff Amos Coaches, a Northamptonshire operator.

Dennis Lancet

Built: Guildford, Surrey 1982-87.
Engines: Perkins 6.354 or V8; Leyland 402, 411; Cummins B.
Transmission: ZF synchromesh, Allison or Voith automatic.
Bodywork: Duple, Alexander, East Lancs, Marshall, Wadham Stringer.
Areas of operation: South Wales, Sunderland, Guildford.
The Lancet, available in 8 to 11m lengths, is a lightweight chassis launched when the Bristol LH was withdrawn. It has a vertical mid-engine, but the high floorline is compensated for by a lower front chassis frame to give a relatively low step entry.

Dennis Javelin

Built: Guildford, Surrey 1987 to date.
Engine: Cummins 6CTA.
Transmission: ZF manual or automatic.
Bodywork: Plaxton, Duple, Wadham Stringer, Wright.
Areas of operation: Norfolk, Suffolk, Co Durham, Winchester, Eastbourne, Shetland.
The medium-weight Javelin is most popular as a coach, but has scored some bus sales. Its compact vertical engine is mounted directly ahead of the rear axle, to maximise luggage space between the axles, and there is an air intake halfway along the offside.

Leyland Leopard

Built: Leyland, Lancashire 1959-82.
Engines: Leyland 0.600, 680; DAF 11.6-litre; Volvo THD100.
Transmission: Leyland or ZF synchromesh; Leyland semi- or fully-automatic.
Bodywork: Alexander, Duple, East Lancs, Marshall, Northern Counties, Plaxton, Willowbrook.
The Leopard is still one of the most common underfloor-engined buses in service. It was especially popular as a bus with SBG companies and some municipal operators in South Wales. Some reconditioned chassis have been rebodied by Willowbrook and Plaxton. A few have been re-powered over the years with DAF and Volvo engines.

Leyland Tiger

Built: Leyland, Lancashire 1982-91.
Engines: Leyland TL11H; Gardner 6HLXB, 6HLXCT; Cummins L10; Volvo THD101.
Transmission: Leyland automatic; ZF automatic or synchromesh.
Bodywork: Alexander, Duple, East Lancs, Plaxton, Reeve Burgess, Wadham Stringer, Wright.

The Tiger was the Leopard's successor with more powerful engines and air suspension to counter competition from Volvo and other importers. It has a front radiator and is capable of taking lower floored bodywork than the Leopard. Some bus versions have leaf springs. Most were built as 11m or 12m vehicles, but Tayside has four 9.5m models with Reeve Burgess bodies. The Cummins engine was standard after Leyland ceased making its own engines, but Ulsterbus/Citybus specified Volvo engines for its more recent deliveries; four Ulster-specification Tigers were delivered to Lowland Omnibuses (ex-SBG) in 1991.

Below:
Leyland DAB: One of South Yorkshire's Danish-built articulated buses with large Continental-size destination screens.

Leyland DAB

Built: Silkeborg, Denmark 1984/85.
Engine: Leyland TL11H.
Transmission: ZF automatic, Leyland semi-automatic.
Areas of operation: Sheffield, Teesside, Leigh (Greater Manchester).
South Yorkshire Transport bought 13 DAB articulated buses in 1985 for special services in Rotherham and Sheffield; they now link the city with the huge Meadowhall Shopping Centre. Their Danish bodies, built using the Alusuisse bolted system, have flat sides, Leyland National-style windscreens and large Continental-style destination screens.

In 1984, Leyland imported two similarly-styled 9.9m DABs, badged as Tiger Cubs, to test the market for post-deregulation buses. The first, now operated by Jim Stones in Greater Manchester, has the same destination screen layout as the artics; the second, operated by Tees and District, was completed by ECW and has the destination screen incorporated into a taller windscreen. Both have single-piece entrance doors.

Leyland Swift

Built: Leyland, Lancashire 1987-91.
Engine: Cummins 6BT.
Transmission: Turner synchromesh, Allison automatic.
Bodywork: PMT, Reeve Burgess, Wadham Stringer, Wright.
The 7.3m and 8.5m Swift was launched soon after Leyland Bus management bought the company from the Rover Group and uses major units from the Leyland DAF Roadrunner 6-10 tonne truck. The vertical engine is mounted behind the front axle and the radiator is directly in front of the engine.

Seddon Pennine 7

Built: Oldham, Lancashire 1973-82.
Engine: Gardner 6HLXB.
Transmission: Fuller synchromesh; Self-Changing Gears semi-automatic.
Bodywork: Alexander, Plaxton, Seddon.
Areas of operation: Glasgow, Edinburgh, Staffordshire, Leicestershire, Devon, Peterborough.
Seddon, then an independent truck builder, developed the Pennine 7 for the SBG as a Gardner-engined alternative to the Leyland Leopard. Over 500 were built, some as coaches. Crosville got one with a Seddon bus body and a few went to independent operators, but SBG's Western and Eastern Scottish fleets took most. Many of the Scottish buses have been sold, some to Stevensons of Uttoxeter.

Volvo B10M, B9M

Built: Boras, Sweden; Irvine, Ayrshire; Workington, Cumbria 1980 to date.
Engine: Volvo THD100, 101.
Transmission: ZF synchromesh or automatic; Self-Changing Gears automatic; Allison automatic.
Bodywork: Alexander, Duple, Caetano, Plaxton, Van Hool, Wadham Stringer, East Lancs, Northern Counties.
The air-sprung B10M and its shorter B9M derivative – successors to the steel-sprung B58 sold in Britain from 1972 — are sold mainly as coaches and not only are the best selling chassis in the UK, but also outsell any mid-engined chassis in Europe. Bus versions, often with relatively low floors, have been built for several operators, including Badgerline, South Yorkshire Transport, Burnley & Pendle and Blackburn Transport. In 1985, West Midlands bought six Scottish-built 11m Citybuses with Alexander bodies. Volvo built B10Ms for UK and other markets at Workington in 1990/91. Volvo has also imported lighter single-deckers, two front-engined B57s and a mid-engined B7M.

CHASSIS — FRONT-ENGINED

Bedford SB/VAS

Built: Dunstable, Bedfordshire 1950-86.
Engines: Bedford diesel and petrol; Perkins diesel.
Transmission: Synchromesh.
Bodywork: Willowbrook, Marshall, Reeve Burgess, Wadham Stringer, Wright.
The 40-seat SB (also known as NJM towards the end of its life) was Britain's longest-lived bus chassis, spanning the period from the end of the postwar travel boom to Bedford's demise as a truck and bus builder. It has a front engine, mounted immediately behind the front axle, next to the driver, with the entrance normally immediately behind the front axle. The smaller VAS, first built in 1961, was a midibus before the term was coined. It takes bodies seating around 30. In later years, it was also known as the PJK.

Ford R-Series

Chassis: Langley, Buckinghamshire 1963-85.
Engine: Ford diesel or petrol.
Transmission: Synchromesh; Allison automatic.
Bodywork: Alexander, Duple, ECW, Marshall, Plaxton, Wadham Stringer, Willowbrook.
Ford's range of 10 and 11m single-deckers first appeared in 1963 as the Thames Trader 676E, but became the R-Series two years later. Until 1977, it had a vertical engine mounted between the driver and the entrance door, ahead of the front axle; for the remaining eight years, the engine was angled to sit below floor level, with the floor ramped up to the front. From 1965 to 1971, 10m models were R192 and 11m were R226; they became R1014 and R1114 respectively in 1971 and R1015 and R1115 in 1982 when a revised engine was fitted. In its heyday, the R-Series was operated by several NBC and SBG fleets. Some of the NBC vehicles were rebuilt as midibuses and a Tricentrol conversion, the T152, was later offered by Ford as a midi bus and coach.

Leyland Cub

Built: Bathgate, West Lothian 1979-86.
Engine: Leyland 98.
Transmission: Turner synchromesh; Allison automatic.
Bodywork: Duple, HTI-Maxeta, Optare, Reeve Burgess, Wadham Stringer.
The Cub was a midibus version of Leyland's Terrier truck and sold better as a welfare/school bus than as a service bus. It has a vertical engine mounted either ahead of the front axle (where the latter is set back) or directly above it.

BODYWORK

In a few cases, buses and coaches have commonly-derived body designs. For the sake of simplicity, some coaches (eg Alexander TC) are shown under the bus heading because the basic body from which they were developed is a bus, but others (eg Duple Dominant E, Van Hool Alizee bus) are derived from coaches and are listed under the coach heading.

Alexander Y-type

Built: Falkirk, Stirlingshire; Mallusk, Co Antrim.
Chassis: Leyland Leopard; Seddon Pennine 7; Bristol RE; Bedford Y-Series; Dennis Lancet; Ford R-Series; Volvo B57; AEC Reliance.
Areas of operation: Throughout Scotland, Co Durham, Leicestershire, Nottinghamshire, Lancashire, Staffordshire.

The first Y-type appeared in 1961, the last (on a Lancet and a B57 for Northern Scottish) in 1982. For most of that period, it was the standard single-decker for SBG companies and it sold to other UK operators, too. A few were built by Alexander's Ulster subsidiary and its predecessor, Potter of Belfast. They have been built from 9.5m to 12m with interior finishes ranging from basic service bus to luxury coach.

   All have the same design of double-curvature windscreen, widening from top to bottom (both single-piece and divided) and the same two-piece rear window which narrows from top to bottom. Front grille designs, always in glass fibre, have changed over the years; Bristols, with front radiators, had larger grilles. The long-windowed version, more often a semi-coach, has three main window bays (four on the few 12m examples), all with gently forward-sloping pillars. The short window version, usually a bus, has vertical windows pillars and twice the number of window bays.

Below:
Alexander Y-type: A long-windowed semi-coach body on a Western Scottish Seddon Pennine 7.

Above:
Alexander Y-type: Rear view of a short-bay bus body on a Kelvin Central Leyland Leopard.

Alexander T-type

Built: Falkirk, Stirlingshire.
Chassis: Leyland Leopard, Tiger; Seddon Pennine 7; Dennis Dorchester.
Areas of operation: Throughout Scotland, South Wales, Nottinghamshire, Northern Ireland.

Below:
Alexander T-type: The original T-type body style, with stepped roof at the front, on a Kelvin Central Leopard semi-coach.

Above:
Alexander TE: A Mansfield & District (Stagecoach group) Leyland Tiger semi-coach with TE body. The TS bus is similar, but has opening windows and bus seats.

Below:
Alexander TC: The coach-style T-type has a plug-type door, swept window lines, a more prominent grille and square windows. This Fife Scottish bus has gasket glazing.

To complement the Y-type with a body better suited to coach work, Alexander created the higher-floor T-type in 1974 and started volume production two years later. The body tapers from the base of the windows, has taller side windows than the Y-type and a flatter roof profile. As built before 1983, it has identical windscreen and rear windows — two-piece curved, narrowing from the bottom and at the front stopping in line with the top of the passenger door — with the destination display set above it. These vehicles have a grille design derived from the Y-type.

In 1983, it was facelifted with a taller windscreen which incorporated a destination display behind the top of the glass, a less elaborate grille confined to the bottom of the front dash and a shallow single-piece rear window. Some older SBG T-types got shallower rear windows. There are three versions of the new T-type: the dual purpose TE; the service bus TS with opening side windows and fewer body mouldings; and the TC coach, with bonded glazing or square or round-edged gasket glazing, single-piece plug type door and further restyled grille. TEs have been exported to the Irish Republic.

Alexander P/PS-type

Built: Falkirk, Stirlingshire.
Chassis: Leyland Tiger; Dennis Lancet, Lance; Volvo B10M; Scania K92, K93, N113; Mercedes-Benz O.405.
Areas of operation: Aberdeen, Dundee, Ayrshire, Newcastle, Nottingham, Nottinghamshire, Derby, West Midlands, South Yorkshire.
The P-type was introduced in 1983 as a Y-type successor and was designed for assembly in overseas markets where Alexander has developed export business. In its original form, it is a very flat-sided design with inward-angled front corner panels and flat windscreens, either one or two-piece with quarterlights. The nearside front corner has either an additional or extended quarterlight for kerbside visibility. The side windows are tall and of the same short length as on the Y-type bus and the grille design, revised on later models, is basic. This style is operated by Bluebird Northern, Fife Scottish, Strathtay Omnibuses, East Midland, Badgerline, West Midlands Travel and Burnley & Pendle.

Below:
Alexander P-type: The angular lines of the original P-type are apparent on this Badgerline Volvo B10M. *Stewart Brown*

Above:
Alexander PS: The radical effect of the rounded front is evident on this Scania K93 in the Derby fleet.

It was superseded in 1988 by the PS-type, first built on Scania K92 chassis. This design has a curved front with tall double-curvature windscreen and integrated destination display. The driver's side window sweeps down to meet the bottom of the windscreen. Operators include Derby, Nottingham, South Yorkshire, Yorkshire Traction, AA Buses and Stevensons. Mercedes-Benz 0.405s will have this body, but with a Mercedes front.

Below:
Alexander (Belfast): The Willowbrook side mouldings are apparent on this Citybus Bristol RELL with the earlier style of Ulster body. *Stephen Morris*

Alexander Belfast body

Built: Mallusk, Co Antrim.
Chassis: Leyland Leopard, Tiger, B21; Bristol RE, LH; Bedford Y-Series.
Areas of operation: Northern Ireland, Ipswich.
In 1968, the year before Alexander (Belfast) was formed, Potters of Belfast started to build a standard body for Ulsterbus single-deckers. From 1973, when the Belfast Corporation undertaking was sold, the same design went to the successor Citybus fleet. When built at Falkirk, the same design was called the PU-type, but it appears to have no name at Mallusk. Its sides, with window bays halfway between the extremes of the Y-type bus and coach in length, are closely akin to contemporary Willowbrook buses, even down to the treatment of side mouldings and the sloping rear window. The front is standard Alexander around the curved windscreen and roof dome, but plainer on the front dash which usually has a substantial bumper. Bristol RELLs have a central emergency exit at the rear and a large front grille.

Alexander N-type, Q-type

Built: Mallusk, Co Antrim.
Chassis: Leyland Tiger, B21; Ford R1015; Volvo B10M.
Areas of operation: Northern Ireland, Ipswich, Greater Manchester, Kent, Darlington, Scottish Borders.
The more aerodynamic N-type body for the Ulster market (including Ford school buses) was introduced in 1984. It has a more angled roofline, an upright rear end, flat P-type windscreens with quarterlights and a square grille. When Shearings (now Timeline) entered the bus market, it standardised on this body for its Leyland Tiger service buses.

In 1990 it was replaced by the Q-type which has a similarly shaped main structure, but a curved front end with a double-curvature divided windscreen which deepens towards the centre. The destination display is integrated into the top. The Q-type has been bought by Shearings, United Auto and Lowland Omnibuses and is available also on Scania K93 and N113 and Dennis Lance chassis.

Below:
Alexander N-type: One of Ipswich's 12m Leyland B21s (badged as a Bristol) with N-type body.

Above:
Alexander Q-type: A Citybus Leyland Tiger with a Q-type body. The deep windscreen and tucked-in lower dash are the most distinctive features. *Stephen Morris*

Below:
Alexander Dash: The prototype Dash, on 8.5m Dennis Dart chassis, painted in the Stagecoach group's Cumberland livery. Stagecoach ordered 321 9.8m and 9.9m Dash bodies on Dart and Volvo B6R chassis in 1991.

Alexander Dash

Built: Falkirk, Stirlingshire.
Areas of operation: Sussex, Cumbria, Glasgow, Inverness
Chassis: Dennis Dart, Volvo B6R.
The Dash is Alexander's body for the new generation of rear-engined midibuses. Its appearance is a marriage of the PS and Q-types, with PS side windows and roof shape and a two-piece double-curvature windscreen which deepens to a point. The destination display is in a separate box above the windscreen. The Stagecoach group placed a launch order for 321 Dash bodies on 9.8m Dart and 9.9m B6R chassis.

BET single-deckers

Bodybuilders: Marshall, Willowbrook.
Chassis: Bristol RE, LH; AEC Reliance, Swift; Leyland Leopard.
From the mid-1960s, Marshall and Willowbrook built a range of near-identical single-deckers to meet the specifications of the BET group, whose bus companies were absorbed into the National Bus Company in 1969. Similar bodies were sold to other customers. They have peaked front and rear roof domes, five window bays (fewer or shorter on 9.5m and 10m versions) and two-piece double-curvature windscreens (the so-called BET windscreens) and rear windows. A key identification point is that Willowbrook bodies have a moulding strap above the windscreen, but Marshall bodies do not.

Below:
BET: An ex-Midland Red Leopard with BET-style **Marshall** body operated by Gibson's of Moffat.

Caetano Stagecoach

Built: Oporto, Portugal.
Chassis: Volvo B10M.
Areas of operation: Glasgow, west London.
Caetano's only venture so far into the UK bus market came in 1985 when it imported the first of four bodies on B10M chassis. It was called the Stagecoach to attract coach operators planning to take advantage of bus deregulation and has semi-coach seats. The shape is reminiscent of the German VöV SLII design. Three Stagecoaches are now operated by Strathclyde Buses, the fourth by Tellings-Golden Miller in west London; two of the Strathclyde buses have gasket-mounted side windows, the others have bonded glazing.

Below:
Caetano Stagecoach: Three of the four Stagecoaches are operated by Strathclyde Buses. This is one of two with gasket-mounted side windows. *Murdoch Currie*

Carlyle Dartline

Built: Blackpool, Lancashire; Birmingham.
Chassis: Dennis Dart.
Areas of operation: London, Watford, Ramsgate, Southampton, North Wales, North Devon, York, Great Yarmouth.
Duple developed the original body for the Dart, using the Cromweld stainless steel construction method pioneered on the 425 coach. Plaxton declined to buy this design with the other Duple products in 1989 and the design was sold instead to Carlyle, a minibus builder formerly owned by NBC, but it went into liquidation in 1991. The body has bonded windows and an S-shaped front with asymmetric barrel-shaped two-piece windscreen, slightly deeper on the nearside. The destination display is integrated into the top of the windscreen of 8.5m and 9m models, on a taller, separate box on 9.8m models; 8.5m and 9.8m models have a shorter window bay in the middle, the 9.8m models having three main windows in the front half. Marshall bought the Carlyle body range in 1992.

Carlyle: A 9.8m Dartline body on a Thanet Bus Dart. The taller destination box is only fitted on long Darts. *Dennis*

Duple Dominant

Built: Blackpool, Lancashire.
Chassis: Bedford Y-series; Bristol LH; Dennis Lancet, Falcon H; Ford R-Series; Leyland Cub, Leopard, Tiger; AEC Reliance; Volvo B10M.
The Dominant bus, built from 1974 to 1987, uses the same pillar spacing as the Dominant coach launched in 1972 and has the same headlamp and grille arrangement as on those original coaches. The arched roof profile, deep destination display area and curved two-piece windscreen was influenced by the Leyland National. The deep side windows are of equal depth except where fitted to Leicester's Falcon Hs and some other lower-floored buses; they have deeper window panes in the two frontmost bays on each side.

Below:
Duple Dominant: A 10m two-door Dominant bus body on a Capital Coaches Ford R1014 operated at Heathrow Airport.

Duple 300

Built: Blackpool, Lancashire.
Chassis: Volvo B10M, Leyland Tiger, Dennis Javelin.
Areas of operation: Co Durham, Norfolk, Suffolk, Essex, Lanarkshire, Northampton, Shetland.
The successor to the Dominant bus, built from 1987 until Duple closed at the end of 1989, is also based on a Duple coach, but externally betrays more of its origins. The 300 is a 3m high version of the 320 coach described on p114 and has the roof profile and lower dash of the coach. It has a wide entrance door and square-edged, gasket-mounted windows which stop short of the roof.

Above:
Duple 300: Unlike the 320 and 340 coaches, the 300 bus has separate body panels between the windows and skirt, to simplify repairs. This is a Leyland Tiger operated by Ralph Bullock of Cheadle in Cheshire.

East Lancs

Built: Blackburn, Lancashire.
Chassis: Bristol LHS, RE; Dennis Dominator, Falcon, Lancet, Lance, Dart; Scania K92; Leyland Leopard, Tiger, Atlantean; Volvo B58, B10M.

Below:
East Lancs: One of the high-window, bowed side bodies on a Scania N112 in the Hull fleet.

Above:
East Lancs: An EL2000 body on a Dennis Falcon HC in the Leicester CityBus fleet. This has curved side windows and windscreen. *Dennis*

Below:
East Lancs: One of Grey-Green's EL2000-bodied short Volvo B10Ms with vee-shaped windscreen and Alexander R-type side windows.

Areas of operation: Burnley, Chesterfield, Accrington, Hartlepool, Lancaster, Ipswich, Leeds, South Wales, Tayside, Southampton, Staffordshire, Merseyside, Blackburn, Bedford, London, Heathrow Airport.

From the mid-1960s, East Lancs built basically flat-sided single-deck bodies with a large rear window to permit reversing. Front ends have graduated from having Alexander-style curved windscreens to a design with flat, two-piece windscreen. Side windows are relatively deep with thin window pillars; roofs, originally rounded, are now tapered in above the window line.

A bow-sided design, initially on Scania chassis, later on Tigers, was launched in 1986. Its flat side windows are set high in the body and windscreens are either deep curved or Alexander-style shallower double-curvature.

In 1990, the aluminium-framed EL2000, also with bow sides, was introduced. It has deeper side windows and a rounded back with a high set rear window similar to Van Hool coaches. Typical of an East Lancs product, there are opportunities for radical variations within the structure and windscreens can be curved or flat vee-shaped. Grey-Green has 20 10.3m and 11m B10Ms with shallower Alexander R-type side windows. A narrower and shorter version is available on Dennis Dart chassis and Southampton Citybus has had Atlantean chassis fitted with new 35-seat EL2000s.

Lex/HTI Maxeta

Built: Southampton, Hampshire.
Chassis: Bedford YMQ/S, Leyland Cub.

The Maxeta body, built first by Lex Vehicle Engineering and later by HTI, is a flat-sided body with angled roofline, an overhanging peaked front dome, flat two-piece windscreen with quarterlights and side windows set higher than the cab window. It was bought by a few NBC companies before minibuses took root.

Below:
Lex Maxeta: A Maxeta body on a Bedford YMQ/S operated by R&I Coaches on the shuttle service between London's Victoria rail and coach stations.

Marshall Camair 80

Built: Cambridge.
Chassis: Dennis Dominator, Falcon, Lancet; Daimler Fleetline; Volvo Ailsa.
Areas of operation: Chester, Chesterfield, Swindon, Darlington, Glasgow.
Marshall launched the Camair 80 in 1978 on Dominators for Darlington and supplied most on Dennis chassis, although four went on older single-deck Fleetline chassis with Tayside and one went to Strathclyde on the only 11m single-deck Ailsa. It has a shallow, arched roof, near flat sides and tall, curved two-piece windscreens with destinational gear built into the top. The front portion of the roof is flat and the leading edge, directly above the windscreen, is scalloped.

Below:
Marshall: A Camair 80 body on one of Darlington's 11m Dennis Dominators. The rear seats are over the rear engine compartment.

Northern Counties

Built: Wigan, Greater Manchester.
Chassis: Dennis Falcon, Domino, Dart; Leyland Leopard; Volvo B10M.
Areas of operation: Ipswich, Hartlepool, Manchester, Leicester, Warrington.
Northern Counties has built relatively few single-deckers. Leopards built in the 1970s and Falcons for Ipswich and Hartlepool are to a style with high set side windows and peaked, flat vee-shaped windscreens. Greater Manchester's Domino midibuses have a variant of this body, with square-edged side windows and taller curved windscreens with integrated destination displays.
   In 1991, it launched the Countybus Paladin on B10M, Dart and Falcon chassis initially. They have square-edged rubber-mounted windows, barrel-shaped two-piece windscreens (shallower on the Dart) and deeper quarterlights.

Top:
Northern Counties: An Ipswich Dennis Falcon H with a style of Northern Counties body built from the early 1970s. Note the distinctive peak-shaped windscreen and high side windows.

Above:
Northern Counties: The prototype Countybus Paladin body, on Volvo B10M chassis, for Greater Manchester Buses. The deep windscreen is barrel-shaped.

Optare

Built: Leeds, West Yorkshire.
Chassis: Dennis Domino, Leyland Cub.
Areas of operation: Stockport, south Manchester, Bristol.
Better known now for its range of complete buses, Optare's first products in 1985 were 14
Dennis Domino midibuses for South Yorkshire. They were followed by 15 Leyland Cubs for
West Yorkshire PTE. The Cubs were resold very quickly and are scattered widely; most of
the Dennises were bought by Stevensons of Uttoxeter. All have front ends with shallow radi-
ators and flat vee-shaped windscreens of Roe style. The Dominos have four-bay bodies, the
Cubs four-and-a-half bays.

Below:
Optare: One of Stevensons, ex-South Yorkshire Dennis Domino midibuses with Optare
bodywork. The ex-West Yorkshire Cubs have a longer version of the same body, but with a
shorter front overhang.

Plaxton Derwent

Built: Scarborough, North Yorkshire.
Chassis: AEC Reliance; Leyland Leopard; Bedford Y-Series; Ford R-Series; Bristol LH.
For many years, Plaxton — like Duple — supplemented its mainstream coach manufacturing with service bus bodies which could be built in summer when demand for coaches had passed its peak. Its earlier Derwent body, built in the 1960s and 1970s, has strong BET influence, notably the double-curvature windscreen and back window and peaked roof domes. West Yorkshire PTE bought them with curved rear domes and a single-piece back window of older design. There is a short side window behind the cab/entrance door on 10m versions and they usually have twin headlamps.

Below:
Plaxton Derwent: An East Surrey Bedford Y-Series with a 10m version of the earlier Derwent body.

Plaxton Bustler

Built: Scarborough, North Yorkshire.
Chassis: Bedford Y-Series; Ford R-Series; Leyland Tiger; Volvo B9M.
The Bustler, built from 1980 to 1986, is a bus version of the Supreme coach and shares its curved side profile and headlamps from the Supreme IV. The side windows are set higher than the cab and run to the roof. As on the Derwent, 10m versions have a short window behind the entrance/cab. It has a BET-style double-curvature windscreen and a large destination screen.

Above:
Plaxton Bustler: A Bustler-bodied Ford R1015 built for operation at Heathrow Airport, hence the offside centre door. The advertisement for Yugoslavian holidays pre-dates the outbreak of civil war in 1991.

Below:
Plaxton Derwent 3000: A 54-seat Leyland Tiger operated by Thames Transit on Oxford city services.

Plaxton Derwent 3000

Built: Scarborough, North Yorkshire.
Chassis: Leyland Leopard, Tiger; Volvo B9M, B10M; Bedford Y-Series; Dennis Javelin.
Areas of operation: Epsom (Surrey), Northampton, Cheltenham, Tyneside, Glasgow, York, Norfolk, Suffolk, Essex, Birmingham, Bedfordshire.
The Derwent 3000, launched in 1986 as the Derwent II, has the same profile as the Bustler, but has shallower, square cornered side windows, a horizontally-divided grille aperture and a wider destination aperture. This body has also been fitted on reconditioned chassis for several operators, including Yorkshire Rider in York.

Plaxton Verde

Built: Scarborough, North Yorkshire.
Chassis: Scania N113, Dennis Lance.
Area of operation: Cardiff.
The aluminium-framed Verde is a total departure from previous Plaxton policy. It was launched in 1991 to reduce the company's reliance on the coach market and is its first purpose designed city bus. It has flat sides with rubber-mounted windows, a high-set rear window and a Continental-style curved front with barrel-shaped divided windscreen, quarterlights and small headlamps.

Below:
Plaxton Verde: A Verde demonstrator, on Scania N113 chassis, in service with SMT. The rearmost side window is shallower to clear the engine compartment. *Stewart J. Brown*

PMT Knype

Built: Stoke-on-Trent, Staffordshire.
Chassis: Leyland Swift; Mercedes-Benz 814.
Areas of operation: Potteries, Isle of Skye.
PMT Engineering developed the angular Knype body in 1987, the first on a rebuilt Mercedes 814 chassis (see minibus section) set-back front axle. One is now operated on the Isle of Skye, but more were built from 1989 on Swift chassis for the PMT operating company. The Knype has square-edged windows which sweep down sharply at the front to meet a deep windscreen.

Below:
PMT Knype: One of PMT's Knype-bodied Leyland Swift 37-seaters. The Knype-bodied Mercedes has a front radiator grille. *Daniel Hill*

Reeve Burgess

Built: Pilsley, Derbyshire.
Chassis: Dennis Dorchester; Bedford SB, VAS; Dodge Commando; Leyland Cub, Tiger; MAN-VW MT 8.136.
Areas of operation: Scottish Borders, Luton airport, Tayside.
A Plaxton subsidiary since 1980, Reeve Burgess specialised in the small bus market, although it also bodied a 12m Dennis Dorchester. Through the 1980s, it built a standard body which began life with a tall, flat two-piece windscreen, but later gained curved windscreens with space above for a destination display. A coach version, the Riviera, has a curved windscreen and bonded side windows; it is fitted on MAN-VW truck chassis and also on four 9.5m shortened Tigers operated by Tayside.

Above:
Reeve Burgess: A Reeve Burgess-bodied Dodge Commando (an adapted truck chassis) on car park duties at Luton Airport. This has a curved windscreen; earlier models have flat windscreens.

Below:
Reeve Burgess: A Pointer body for Rossendale on a 9m Dennis Dart. It has a split step arrangement to comply with the standards laid down by Greater Manchester PTE for its tendered services. *Reeve Burgess*

Reeve Burgess Pointer

Built: Pilsley, Derbyshire; Scarborough, North Yorkshire.
Chassis: Dennis Dart, Volvo B6R.
Areas of operation: London, Barnsley, Chester, Southampton, Bromley (Kent), Sheffield.
Beneath the skin, the aluminium-framed Pointer is a scaled down Plaxton Verde. It was developed jointly by Reeve Burgess and Plaxton and was being built at Scarborough in 1991 some weeks before it was decided to close the Pilsley factory and combine all midibus, bus and coach production under one roof. The Pointer has square-edged gasket glazing, with a half-bay on 8.5m and 9.8/9.9m versions, a double-curvature windscreen and doors with separate top and bottom glazing.

Wadham Stringer Vanguard

Built: Waterlooville, Hampshire.
Chassis: Dennis Falcon, Dorchester, Lancet, Lance, Javelin; Scania N112; Ward Dalesman GRXI; Bedford Y-Series, SB, VAS: Bristol LHS; Leyland Tiger, Cub, Swift; Volvo B57, B58.
Areas of operation: Grimsby, Manchester, Hartlepool, Newport, Darlington, Ayrshire, Cambridge, Eastbourne, Watford, Hitchin, Bristol, Harrogate, Heathrow Airport.
Wadham Stringer was already established in the ambulance and defence markets when it began to tackle the bus market in 1979 with the Vanguard body. It sold well to municipal operators in the early days. The design has slightly inward-sloping flat sides, deep side windows with narrow pillars, a slightly arched double-curvature windscreen with a more arched roof dome to accommodate the destination screen, a low, horizontal grille and a small roof pod at the rear. The Vanguard II, launched in 1986 and particularly popular for a time on Leyland Swift chassis, has square edged windows and a more rounded lower dash panel. A coach version for the Swift, called the Winchester, was launched in 1989. It has a single piece windscreen and non-opening side windows.

Above:
Wadham Stringer: An all-white Vanguard II-bodied Leyland Swift in service with Luton & District in Hitchin.

Wadham Stringer Portsdown

Built: Waterlooville, Hampshire.
Chassis: Dennis Dart; ACE Cougar.
Areas of operation: Eastbourne, Portsmouth, Leigh (Greater Manchester), Croydon.
Wadham Stringer was the first bodybuilder to offer an alternative to the Carlyle/Duple
Dartline body for the Dart. In many ways, it is a reaction against some of the less popular
features of the original. It is steel framed, with gasket-mounted square-edged side windows
and a double-curvature divided windscreen. It has a half-bay central window in 8.5m form
and also was built on the prototype ACE Cougar for People's Provincial. Dart customers
include Eastbourne, Jim Stones of Glazebury and East Surrey.

Below:
Wadham Stringer: A 9m Portsdown-bodied Dennis Dart operated by Jim Stones in Leigh,
Greater Manchester.

Willowbrook 001

Built: Loughborough, Leicestershire.
Chassis: Bedford Y-series; Ford R-Series.
As well as building BET-style bodies on heavy-duty chassis, Willowbrook developed a parallel product for lightweight chassis in the mid-1960s. After the company was bought out of Duple ownership in 1971, the body was christened 001. It has deeper side windows than on the BET body, has a large grille derived from that used on Duple coaches of the early 1960s and, in original form, has a sloping rear end with a large single window. Later models have an upright rear with two-piece BET double-curvature window.

Below:
Willowbrook 001: Typical of later versions of the 001 body is this Bedford YMT operated in Newcastle by Andersons of Westerhope. It has plain side mouldings; earlier models have the more elaborate mouldings also used at the time by Alexander (Belfast). *Kevin Lane*

Willowbrook Warrior

Built: Loughborough, Leicestershire.
Chassis: Leyland Leopard; Bedford Y-Series; ACE Cougar.
Areas of operation: Oxford, Maidstone, Nottingham, Lewes, Dunbartonshire, Stirlingshire, West Wales, Solihull, Greater Manchester.
The 1971 Willowbrook was a casualty of the early 1980s recession, but was reformed on a smaller scale in 1985. Since its launch in 1987, the Warrior has established a niche for itself, particularly as a low cost new bus body for reconditioned coach chassis. It is similar in shape to the Leyland Lynx, has square or round-edged rubber-mounted side windows and has a flat, divided windscreen.

Above:
Willowbrook Warrior: City of Oxford has had several Duple and ECW-bodied Leyland Leopard coaches fitted with new Warrior bodies. They have square-edged gasket-mounted windows; some others have rounded windows.

Below:
Wright TT: A narrow-width TT body on a Bedford SB built for operation in Jersey, but operated from new by Myalls of Bassingbourn and photographed on a Cambridge city service.

Wright TT

Built: Ballymena, Co Antrim.
Chassis: Bedford SB, Y-Series; Leyland Leopard.
Areas of operation: Northern Ireland, Maidstone, Cambridge.
The flat-sided TT body uses the Alusuisse construction system also used by Optare and DAB and has also been sold extensively on welfare and school buses in Northern Ireland and Scotland. Its most distinctive feature is its three-piece wedge-shaped windscreen which can be square or round-edged. Apart from two Leopards for Ulsterbus (one of them a coach branded Royale), all TTs have been Bedfords.

Wright Handybus

Built: Ballymena, Co Antrim.
Chassis: Dennis Dart, Leyland Swift.
Areas of operation: London, Walsall, Tyneside, Staffordshire.
There is a look of a 1950s bus on Wright's Alusuisse body for the Dart. It is a unique square design with an option of either separate windscreens with the driver's screen raked back like the Lynx, or a single piece flat screen. It has a central half-bay on 8.5m chassis, but has longer windows on 9m and 9.8m models. London Buses was its main initial customer, but West Midlands Travel and Go-Ahead Northern have also placed orders and Stevensons has four higher versions on Swift chassis.

Below:
Wright Handybus: The tight turning circle of the Dart is demonstrated by this Wright-bodied 8.5m model in London Buses' Centrewest fleet. It has separate windscreens. Note the Wright's W-shaped grille between the small headlamps.

PART 3 COACHES

Coaches are most readily identified by their coachwork, rather than by the chassis, and are listed accordingly. In many cases, the chassis is hard to recognise, but for the sake of completeness, the following is a summary of separate chassis used as the basis of coaches.

BUS CHASSIS ALSO USED AS COACHES:

Rear-engined:

Bristol RE; Dennis Falcon V (longitudinal Perkins V8 engine); MAN 11.180 (and lighter 10.180); Scania K92, K93; Volvo B6R.

Mid-engined:

AEC Reliance; Bedford Y-Series, Venturer; Bristol LH; Dennis Dorchester, Lancet, Javelin, Leyland Leopard, Tiger, Swift; Seddon Pennine 7; Volvo B58, B10M, B9M.

Front-engined:

Bedford SB, VAS; Ford R-Series.

CHASSIS BUILT EXCLUSIVELY AS COACHES

Rear-engined

DAF SB2300/2305
Built: Eindhoven, Netherlands 1980 to date.
Engine: DAF 8.25 litre.
Transmission: ZF synchromesh or automatic.
Length: 12m two-axle.
DAF SB3000
Built: Eindhoven, Netherlands 1985 to date.
Engine: DAF 11.6 litre.
Transmission: ZF synchromesh or automatic.
Length: 12m two or three-axle.
IVECO 315
Built: Flumeri, Italy 1985-90.
Engine: Iveco 5.5 litre.
Transmission: ZF synchromesh.
Length: 7.3m two-axle.
MAN 16.290 HOCL
Built: Salzgitter, Germany 1989 to date.
Engine: MAN D2066 12 litre.
Transmission: ZF synchromesh.
Length: 12m two-axle.
MERCEDES-BENZ O.303
Built: Mannheim, Germany 1975-91.
Engine: Mercedes OM402 V8.
Transmission: Mercedes synchromesh or automatic; ZF synchromesh.
Length: 12m two-axle.

QUEST 80 VM and C
Built: Telford, Shropshire 1984.
Engine: Ford 2726T.
Transmission: Ford synchromesh.
Length: 9-12m two-axle.
SCANIA K112/K113
Built: Katrineholm, Sweden 1982 to date (K113 from 1988).
Engine: Scania DS11 (DSC11 on K113) 11 litre.
Transmission: Scania synchromesh, automatic.
Length: 12m two or three-axle.

Mid-engined

ACE PUMA
Built: Huddersfield, West Yorkshire 1984-86 (rear-engined version built 1988).
Engines: Perkins T6; DAF 8.25 litre.
Transmission: ZF synchromesh.
Length: 8m two-axle
DAF MB200/MB230
Built: Eindhoven, Netherlands 1975 to date.
Engine: DAF 11.6 litre.
Transmission: ZF synchromesh or automatic.
Length: 11m or 12m two-axle.
WARD DALESMAN
Built: Huddersfield, West Yorkshire 1982-84.
Engine: Perkins TV8, Cummins 6CTA.
Transmission: ZF synchromesh.
Length: 11m or 12m two-axle.

COACH BODIES AND INTEGRALS

Berkhof

Built: Valkenswaard, Netherlands.
Chassis: AEC Reliance; DAF SB2300, 3000, MB200; Dennis Dorchester, Javelin; Iveco 315; Leyland Tiger; Scania K92, K112, K113; Volvo B10M; MAN 11.180.
Berkhof bodies were first imported to Britain in 1982 by Ensign Bus Sales in Essex and sold especially well to operators in southern England. The range built shares a gently bowed side treatment, with windows running to roof level, a raked-back windscreen and an upswept grille/headlamp assembly. Smallest in the range is the Elk midicoach; next up the 3.5m high Esprite with single-piece or vertically-divided windscreen; then the 1½-deck 3.95m Emperor which has the main seating built above the driver's cab, an additional seating area behind the rear axle and a horizontally-divided, taller windscreen; and largest is the 4m Eclipse double-decker which has separate upper and lower windscreens.

The 1987 Excellence range was introduced to the UK in 1989 on Scania, Volvo, MAN and Dennis Javelin chassis when AVE Berkhof took over the franchise. This has a revised front end with twin recessed headlamps. The 3.3m Excellence 1000 has a single-piece double-curvature windscreen, the 3.7m 2000 has a horizontally divided windscreen, the bottom half of which is upright and the top half is raked. The 2000 front has a hint of Neoplan styling. A 4m 2000 double-decker on DAF SB3000 chassis, was imported in 1988.

Above:
Berkhof: An Eclipse-bodied DAF SB3000 typifies the style of body, with upswept mouldings round the headlamps, sold in the UK from 1982.

Below:
Berkhof: One of the first Excellence bodies to be imported was this 2000-bodied Volvo B10M for Moor Dale, a subsidiary of the Proudmutual group which also owns Northumbria and Kentish Bus. *AVE Berkhof*

Bova Europa

Built: Valkenswaard, Netherlands 1981-83.
Engine: DAF 8.25 litre.
Transmission: ZF synchromesh or Allison automatic.
The integral Bova was one of the first successful imports of a rear-engined Continental coach to Britain and sold well to smaller operators which had previously bought lightweight Bedfords and Fords. The sides and rear are flat, with glazing to roof level. The roof slopes down to the front, which has a large two-piece double-curvature windscreen, a curved front and shallow grille. The front axle has a narrow track. The Europa underframe was also bodied by Duple.

Below:
Bova Europa: The square sides, prominent curved front and narrow track front axle all help to identify the first Bova for the UK.

Bova Futura

Built: Valkenswaard, Netherlands 1983 to date.
Engine: DAF 11.6 litre.
Transmission: ZF synchromesh.
The Europa gave way to the more powerful and radically styled Futura which is available in 3.3m and 3.5m versions. It is more aerodynamic, with gently bowed sides, a raked-back windscreen and a bulbous front dash panel which tucks back into the bottom. The front grille is a slatted area at the frontmost part of the front dash.

Above:
Bova Futura: The shape of the Futura is unmistakable, a styling feature which also contributes to fuel economy. The offside Continental door is halfway along the coach.

Caetano

Built: Oporto, Portugal.

Chassis: Bedford Y-Series; Ford R-Series; Leyland Tiger; Volvo B58, B10M, B6R; DAF MB200/230, SB2300, SB3000; Dennis Dorchester, Javelin; MAN 10.180; Toyota Coaster; Iveco 79.14 truck.

Caetano led the march of imported coach bodies into Britain, when it started selling here in 1968. From 1978 to 1982, it sold the square profile Alpha identifiable by its rear roof pod and forward sloping rear end.

In 1973, it gave way to the Algarve, with bowed sides and deep, single-piece raked-back windscreen. Originally, it had a shallow grille with arrow-shaped vertical slats, but by 1986 the slats were horizontal. Late in 1991, the Algarve II was brought to Britain. It has a more raked front with horizontally divided windscreen on 3.5m and 3.7m models, upswept cab and entrance door glazing and revamped interior.

Caetano is 27% owned by Toyota and builds its Optimo 21-seat midicoach on the Japanese manufacturer's Coaster chassis, the world's best selling bus. It has deep windows all round and its front axle, which has independent suspension, is set back slightly, but still ahead of the entrance door. Models sold from the UK launch in 1985 until 1990 have an upright profile with side windows which step down to meet the windscreen and step up to meet the back window. The successor Optimo II is more powerful and has a rounded profile, with raked back windscreen and back and side windows which sweep up from windscreen to rear window level. In 1985, Caetano also imported a derivative of the Optimo, the Viana. It is based on the Iveco 79.14 truck and has its front axle set back to accommodate a narrow entrance on the front overhang.

Above:
Caetano: An Alpha-bodied Ford R-Series. Note the roof pod at the back.

Below:
Caetano: An Algarve-bodied DAF with horizontal slats between the headlamps. This is a lower floor version; high-floor models have a horizontally-divided windscreen.

Above right:
Caetano: A 3.5m Algarve II on a DAF SB3000 chassis. The window pillars are in the body colour, rather than matt black and the paint scheme emphasises the swept lines of the cab window.

Right:
Caetano: The original style of Optimo, with upright profile and stepped window lines. The Viana body is similar, but the front axle is set back further.

Below right:
Caetano: An Optimo II, with raked front and back, flowing window lines and gasket-mounted windscreen.

Carrosserie Lorraine

Built: Fourchambault, France.
Chassis: Iveco 315.
Plaxton bought Carrosserie Lorraine, a small French coachbuilder, from Iveco in 1988 and late in 1989 brought a small batch of Iveco 315 midicoaches into Britain. They have bowed sides, raked fronts and large single-piece windscreens.

Below:
Carrosserie Lorraine: Skye-Ways is the operator of one of the few Iveco 315 midicoaches imported from Plaxton's French subsidiary. Just visible to the left is part of a PMT Knype-bodied Mercedes 814. *Stewart Brown*

Delta Plan

Built: Lieto, Finland.
Chassis: Scania K112; Volvo B10MT.
Delta Plan bodies, built by a subsidiary of the Finnish Ajokki group, are rare in the UK. High floor vehicles, they are identifiable by their heavily curved side windows and horizontally-divided, raked windscreens.

Delta Plan: One of the rare Finnish-built coaches, with tall heavily curved sides, on a three-axle Volvo B10MT chassis. The 'T' in the chassis designation is for the extra, 'tandem' axle. *Colin Martin*

Duple Dominant

Built: Blackpool, Lancashire.
Chassis: AEC Reliance; Bedford VAS, SB, Y-Series; Ford R Series; Dennis Falcon V; Leyland Leopard, Tiger; Volvo B58, B10M; DAF MB200.
Duple followed Plaxton styling with its 1972 Dominant, but stole a march on its rival by switching to steel framing in place of composite (metal and wood) used before. It has

---

Duple Dominant: A Dominant II-bodied Bedford YMT. The Dominant I's windscreen and cab window stop in line with the bottom of the side windows; Dominant E bus versions have less chrome brightwork below the windows and on the lower panels.

Above:
Duple Dominant: The forward-sloping small windows help identify a Dominant III. It has a Dominant I windscreen to accommodate the 'Bristol dome' destination box which carries the operator's name.

Above right:
Duple Dominant: A Midland Scottish Super Goldliner-bodied Leyland Tiger with a straight front roof dome and deeper windscreen. It began life with Dominant III windows, but was rebuilt with Dominant II side windows.

---

bowed sides, brightwork window surrounds (usually including a ribbed section under the windows) and, in its original form, interchangeable vertically-divided windscreen and rear windows. A bus-seated version, the Dominant E, was offered from 1975 with less brightwork; both models were available with a 'Bristol dome' (so called after Plaxton bodied REs for NBC companies) destination display above the windscreen.

The Michelotti-styled Dominant II, with deeper windscreen, restyled grille (also introduced on the original body) and shallower single-piece windscreen was available from 1976 on underfloor-engined coaches and on inclined-engine Fords from 1977.

To meet SBG's requirements for overnight coaches, the Dominant III was developed in 1980. It had small, forward-sloping trapezoid windows similar to those on SBG's Alexander M-type coaches built from 1968. At the same time, the Dominant IV, with shallower standard-shaped windows and much less brightwork, became available. The Goldliner high-floor versions of the Dominant II, III and IV, with roofline either stepped behind the cab/entrance or run straight through behind a destination screen, were launched in 1981, the year before Dominant production stopped.

There were further variations: Dominant II, III and IV with Dominant I windscreens; Dominant II with Dominant I rear window; and Dominant II side windows in the front half and Dominant IV windows in the back half. Flat glasses were also available and some SBG Dominant IIIs have been rebuilt with Dominant II and IV side windows.

All models were available with either a single-piece inward-hinging door (some Goldliners have outward-opening plug doors), but for local service work, they were built with two-leaf doors, all-glass in the early days, later metal with four separate window panes.

Duple Laser

Built: Blackpool, Lancashire.
Chassis: Bedford Y-Series; Leyland Tiger; Volvo B10M.
The Dominant's low-floor successor, built from 1982 to 1985, looks similar, but has a more acutely raked front. For its first two years, it was built with a divided windscreen and round-edged, gasket-mounted side windows; for its final year — after Dennis's then parent, Hestair, bought the company — it gained a single-piece windscreen, revised grille and square-edged bonded side windows. Where fitted, destination displays are built into the top of the windscreen.

Below:
Duple Laser: An early Laser-bodied Leyland Tiger, with divided windscreen and gasket glazing, operating on a Maidstone & District London commuter service.

Above:
Duple Caribbean: A later model Caribbean-bodied Tiger, with single-piece windscreen, restyled grille and bonded glazing, in London Coaches' fleet.

Below:
Duple Calypso: The lower Calypso has wider window pillar spacing to match the Bova chassis mountings. Note also the narrow track front axle. Greenslades is a former NBC company now part of a larger Devon coach company.

Duple Caribbean/Calypso

Built: Blackpool, Lancashire.
Chassis: Leyland Tiger; Volvo B10M; Dennis Dorchester; DAF MB200; Bova.
The Dominant's high-floor successor, the Caribbean, has almost flat sides, square-edged side windows and a deep windscreen. Like the Laser, it had a short life and for its last year gained bonded glazing and a restyled grille. The lowheight Calypso, built exclusively on Bova chassis, was sold in 1984/85. It has five window bays instead of six and is further identifiable by its narrow track front axle.

Duple 425

Built: Blackpool, Lancashire 1985-89; Fourchambault, France 1992.
Engines: Cummins L10; DAF 10.6 litre.
Transmission: ZF synchromesh or automatic.
When Hestair bought Duple in 1983, it was developing an integral Caribbean on a Neoplan chassis and the project developed into the distinctive 12m integral 425 which was launched at the 1984 Motor Show, a year before production began. It uses the Cromweld construction system subsequently used on the Dartline bus body and, mechanically, has air suspension and a rear engine. To achieve the 0.425 drag coefficient from which the model number is derived, the windscreen, with deep glazing, is raked back sharply into the roof dome. Three were exported to Switzerland and, after Plaxton bought the Duple coach designs in 1989, it re-engineered the vehicle and built 12 at the Lorraine plant before it closed.

Below:
Duple 425: A 425, with unmistakable raked roof dome, operating with The Bee Line on the Railair Link from Heathrow Airport to Reading.

Duple 340: The higher of the 300-Series coaches has a sloping roof dome and lower cab window and entrance door.

BIRMINGHAM   322

NATIONAL EXPRESS

20   NATIONAL EXPRESS

C120 GKH

Duple 320/340

Built: Blackpool, Lancashire; Scarborough, North Yorkshire.
Chassis: Bedford Y-Series; Leyland Tiger; Volvo B10M; DAF MB, SB; Scania K93; Dennis Javelin.

The Laser and Caribbean gave way in 1985 to the 3.2m high 320 and the 3.4m 340, both of which bear a passing resemblance to the Caribbean. They have flat sides, raked back single or vertically-divided windscreens and bonded glazing. The 340's unglazed front roof dome has a hint of the 425, but is less dramatic. Plaxton built a further 25 320 bodies, all on Tiger chassis, at the end of 1990. These are badged as the Plaxton 321 and have Plaxton-designed interiors, wheelarch and side mouldings.

Below:
Plaxton 321: One of the 25 Scarborough-built versions of the 320 body on a Leyland Tiger chassis, many of which went to Welsh operators including Thomas of Tonypandy. It has Plaxton 321 badging on the grille.

ECW

Built: Lowestoft, Suffolk.
Chassis: Leyland Leopard, Tiger.

ECW revived a 1970 body style in 1982 when it built most of the coaches for NBC companies that year. The design, coded B51 by Leyland, has flat side windows and a high-set windscreen with destination screen built into the top. When new, the area immediately below the windscreen was painted matt black to create an illusion of a deeper glazed area. Structural problems plagued these vehicles, which were designed originally for the Bristol RE, and many have since been rebodied.

Above:
ECW: A City of Oxford Leopard with ECW B51 body. When new many of these vehicles had the mouldings below the windscreen painted black to make the glazed area look deeper.

FAP-Sanos S315.21 Charisma

Built: Skopje, Yugoslavia.
Engine: Mercedes-Benz OM442 V8.
Transmission: ZF synchromesh.

The Charisma is a low cost version of the Mercedes-Benz O.303, licence-built in Yugoslavia. Ensign Bus Sales imported it in 1989/90 after severing ties with Berkhof, selling it at around two-thirds of the price of the German original. It is barely distinguishable from a 'real' O.303, save for the badging, but even then some operators have replaced the circular front badge with the Mercedes three-pointed star. Customers included Shearings and Stagecoach-owned United Counties.

Below:
Charisma: One of Shearings' Yugoslavian-built Mercedes O.303 look-alikes. This one is badged genuinely, but several have had Mercedes three-pointed stars fitted between the headlamps. *Kevin Lane*

Ikarus Blue Danube

Built: Budapest, Hungary.
Chassis: Volvo B10M.

Ikarus's first foray into the UK market came in 1987 when the Kirkby coach and bus dealer-ship imported the first of 101 Blue Danube bodies designed for western markets. The deal was reached before Kirkby management bought Plaxton. The 3.6m Blue Danube has bowed side windows, a tall windscreen and a front dash which tucks in towards the bottom, beneath the shallow main part of the grille. Among the last Blue Danubes sold from Kirkby's stock were five for Thames Transit's Oxford-London service; Colchester Borough Transport is another customer.

Below:
Ikarus: A Blue Danube-bodied Volvo B10M operated by Thames Transit on its Oxford Tube London-Oxford service.

Irizar

Built: San Sebastian, Spain.
Chassis: Volvo B10M.

Irizar (pronounced 'Ireethar') bodies are built by a Basque co-operative and have been imported in small numbers since 1979. Since 1983, a Scottish dealer has imported the 3.5m Pyrenean and 3.4m Shetland bodies distinguishable by their upswept rear side windows and bowed sides. Tayside probably uses more than any other operator.

Above:
Irizar: One of Tayside's Pyrenean-bodied Volvo B10Ms, with upswept rear window, operating on contract to Caledonian Express, the National Express brand name for the express services it bought from Stagecoach in 1989. *Derek Hall*

Jonckheere

Built: Roeslare, Belgium.
Chassis: Bedford, Y-Series; Volvo B58, B10M; Leyland Tiger; DAF SB, MB; Scania K112; Dennis Lancet; Quest 80 C; MAN 11.180, 16.290.

Below:
Jonckheere: A Bermuda-bodied Volvo, with tall grille and relatively shallow windscreen.

Above:
Jonckheere: On these coaches operated by Scancoaches of London, the grille and lower dash is the main distinguishing feature between the Deauville-bodied Volvo B10M on the left and the P599 Jubilee-bodied Scania on the right. P50 Jubilee bodies have tall vertically divided windscreens.

Jonckheere (pronounced 'Yonk here') has been building for the UK market since the early 1970s, most seriously since 1980. The Bermuda, with high floor, square-edged bonded side windows in a gently curved side profile, high set two-piece double-curvature windscreen, higher set single-piece rear window and large rectangular grille, lasted until 1982.

It was superseded by the Jubilee range of high-floor, half-deck and double-deck coaches. These all have a shallower grille with the manufacturer's 'J' badge, square headlamps and curved windscreen. Base model is the 3.5m P50 with side windows which start in line with the roof and top of the windscreen and stop before the bottom of the windscreen; the P599 has a lower driving position and a deeper, horizontally divided windscreen (which can also be vertically divided in the bottom half); the 4m P90 and P95 have an additional rear compartment behind the rear axle (the P95 is on three-axle chassis); the P99 4m double-decker has separate upper and lower windscreens and is on three-axle Scania K112 and DAF SB chassis. Additionally, a few P35 Piccolo midicoach bodies were built on Quest 80 C chassis.

The P599 Deauville design, with restyled front, replaced the Jubilee in 1989. It has been built on B10M, DAF SB3000 and MAN chassis. A P99 double-deck version is offered on MAN and DAF chassis.

LAG

Built: Bree, Belgium.
Chassis: DAF MB200; Volvo B10M; Leyland Tiger; Integral.
The first LAG Galaxy bodies came to Britain in 1982. They have raked fronts with single or two-piece windscreens which sweep up to meet the side glazing.

By 1987, LAG had switched to integral construction and was selling the Panoramic model in the UK. It has ZF gearbox and a choice of either DAF 11.6 litre or (less common) Cummins L10 engine. The front is more upright and the windscreen horizontally divided, but still with the upswept lines of the Galaxy windscreen.

In an immense gamble, LAG moved to a new factory in 1989 and replaced the Panoramic with the DAF-engined 3.6m Eos integral with independent front suspension. It has separate upper and lower windscreens and deep, black mouldings around the high-set headlamps to create an illusion of deeper glazing. LAG's gamble drove it into the hands of rival Van Hool in 1990. It is continuing to build the Eos, including an Eos 200 version with horizontally-divided windscreen.

Top:
LAG Galaxy: The raked front and sweeping lines of the windscreen help identify the Galaxy body on this DAF.

Above:
LAG Panoramic: The down-swept windscreen is retained, but the front is more upright on the integral Panoramic.

Above:
LAG Eos: An early UK market Eos, showing the separate windscreens. Black mouldings make the driver's windscreen appear much lower. Van Hool now sells this model as the Eos 100. *Stephen Morris*

Below:
Leyland Royal Tiger Doyen: Continental styling influenced Leyland when it designed the body for the Royal Tiger. The badge is a Tiger with a crown.

Leyland Royal Tiger Doyen

Built: Leeds, West Yorkshire 1982-84; Workington, Cumbria 1982-88.
Engines: Leyland TL11H; Cummins L10.
Transmission: Leyland automatic, ZF synchromesh, automatic.
Outside bodywork: Plaxton, Van Hool.

The rear-engined Royal Tiger was Leyland's final answer to the flood of foreign coaches which hit the UK around 1980. When bodied in-house, first by Roe, but mainly at Workington, it was called the Doyen, It has a deep, raked windscreen made to appear even deeper by the black ribbed moulding beneath it. The bonded side windows curve sharply at the top. The few underframes bodied by Plaxton and Van Hool are identifiable by air intakes around the engine compartment. Volvo axed the Royal Tiger when it bought Leyland Bus in 1988.

MAN SR280

Built: Salzgitter, Germany (for UK) 1979-85.
Engine: MAN 11.4 litre.
Transmission: ZF synchromesh.

The SR280 was the first high specification rear-engined Continental coach offered in quantity to UK operators. It was offered in higher and lower forms, with flat sides and a choice of vertically-divided or single-piece windscreen. The rectangular grille is an MAN hallmark.

Below:
MAN SR280: MAN integrals are unlike any other coaches on British roads. This is a lower height model with single-piece windscreen.

MCW Metroliner

Built: Birmingham, West Midlands 1982-87.
Engines: Cummins L10; Gardner 6LYT.
Transmission: Voith or ZF automatic, ZF synchromesh.

MCW launched itself into the coach market in 1982 with the 12m Metroliner, of which 130 double-deckers and 42 single-deckers were built.

The most common version, some of which still operate with Armstrong Galley, West Midlands Travel and National Express, is the 4.2m three-axle double-decker with transverse Cummins L10 engine. It has bonded side windows, curved on the top deck, deep wraparound windscreens on both decks, usually divided, a large rear luggage area and either one or two plug-type doors. The last three double-deckers, built in 1986/87, are fully integral 4m 400GT models with longitudinal Gardner engines and heavily raked fronts.

The single-deckers have longitudinal L10 engines. Half were 3.2m with separate chassis, half 3.4m integral Hi-Liners. The first 11 3.2m models had square, flat-sides bodies with bonded glazing and a slightly curved asymmetrical windscreen. The rest have a restyled body with curved wide windows and a raked windscreen. The Hi-Liner has a separate panel for the destination indicator above the windscreen and a deeper panel above the rear entrance door.

Below:
MCW Metroliner: An Ambassador Travel 4.2m double-decker operating on a London-East Anglia service for National Express.

Above right:
MCW Metroliner: One of West Midlands Travel's 4m 400GT double-deckers, identifiable by the heavily raked upper windscreen and swept-down lower deck windows. *Stephen Morris*

Right:
MCW Metroliner: East Kent has built up a fleet of Metroliner single-deckers new and second-hand. This is one of the original style, with square body and slightly asymmetric windscreen.

Below right:
MCW Metroliner: Another East Kent coach, a former demonstration model Hi-Liner, with the curved lines of the later body. The 3.2m version lacks the mouldings above the door.

Mercedes-Benz O.303

Built: Mannheim, Germany 1975-90.
Engine: Mercedes-Benz OM442 V8.
Transmission: Mercedes-Benz synchromesh.
Mercedes first brought its O.302 integral to Britain in 1967, but it took until 1985 for serious imports of the O.303 to begin. The shape is familiar to travellers throughout Europe — and beyond — with its short, curved side windows, deep single-piece or divided windscreen and three-pointed star logo between the headlamps. Padane, Jonckheere and Plaxton-bodied O.303s have also been sold in Britain, several with Mercedes windscreens and front dash, and Plaxton built 25 with standard Paramount 3500 bodies in 1990. Production of the O.303 is being transferred to Moscow and the 1991 O.404 successor will eventually be sold in the UK.

Below:
Mercedes-Benz O.303: One of the last complete O.303s sold in the UK, this high-floor Kings Ferry coach is used for prestige private hires and Kent-London commuter services. It has a single-piece windscreen.

Neoplan

Built: Stuttgart and Berlin, Germany 1980 to date (for UK).
Engines: Mercedes-Benz OM422 V8, OM423 V10; Gardner 6LYT; Cummins 14 litre; Scania DS11; DAF 11.6 litre.
Transmission: ZF synchromesh or automatic; Scania automatic.
The highly individual Neoplan range of exotically-styled integral coaches has become firmly established on the UK market and has succeeded the Metroliner as National Express's double-deck coach; the importer is now a National Express subsidiary. The most common and most ostentatious is the N122 Skyliner double-decker — a three-axle, 12m long, 4m high

model with Mercedes V10, Gardner or Cummins engine. It has forward-sloping window pillars on both decks, curved upper deck windows and a raked upper deck windscreen. The Mercedes V8-engined 3.5m N116 Cityliner and N117 Spaceliner single-deckers have low driving positions and windscreens with raked top halves; the N117 has seats above the driver. Most conventional is the 3.4m N216 Jetliner, with Scania, DAF or Mercedes engines, which has a driving position only slightly lower than the passenger area. All three have curved side windows. In 1991, two Berlin-built N316 Transliners with Mercedes V8 engines were brought to Britain to test the market. They are cheaper then the Stuttgart range and styled more plainly, with more gently bowed sides, but standard Neoplan lower front dash.

Below:
Neoplan: An N122 Skyliner on an Anglo-Scottish motorway service. Many Skyliners have single-piece windscreens and later models have a restyled dash with raised headlamps.

Bottom:
Neoplan: The Transliner body has none of the flamboyance of the rest of the range, but the lower dash and headlamp arrangements are similar to those on newer examples of the main range. *Stewart J. Brown*

Padane

Built: Italy.
Chassis: Volvo B10M; Leyland Tiger; Mercedes-Benz O.303.
Ensign Bus Sales imported a few highly distinctive Padane bodies in the early 1980s. Distinctive features are the flat sides with raked windscreen and first window bay and the sloping roof over the cab and first bay. Padane constructions have a ribbed aluminium panel around the middle of the body.

Below:
Padane: The almost serpent-like lines of the Padane body are evident on this Volvo B10M.

Plaxton Panorama Elite

Built: Scarborough, North Yorkshire.
Chassis: AEC Reliance; Bedford Y-Series; Ford R-Series; Leyland Leopard; Volvo B58; Bristol LH, RE.
Plaxton set a new trend in 1968 when it launched the bow-sided Panorama Elite with two-piece curved windscreen and rear windows, round-edged side windows and ribbed skirt, On 11m and 12m bodies, there is a short window immediately behind the entrance on the nearside. Before 1974, the offside emergency door was directly behind the driver's cab, but for 1974/75 it was moved to just behind the rear axle. For local service work, the Elite Express, with wider two-piece doors, was launched in 1970.

Above:
Plaxton Panorama Elite: The beading above the side windows, the ribbed skirt and wide, shallow grille help identify the Elite body on an AEC Reliance operating a local bus service in Rotherham.

Plaxton Supreme and Viewmaster

Built: Scarborough, North Yorkshire.
Chassis: AEC Reliance; Bedford Y-Series, VAS, SB; Ford R-Series; Leyland Leopard, Tiger; Volvo B58, B10M; Bristol LH; DAF MB, SB; Seddon Pennine 7; Mercedes-Benz O.303; Ward Dalesman.

Plaxton began to introduce all-metal bodies when it launched the Supreme in 1974. Compared with the Elite, it has taller side windows which curve into the roofline. There is no beading above the side windows, the windscreen and rear window are more pointed on models built before 1980 and the grille is taller to avoid fitting extra slats for vehicles like the LH and Ford which have front radiators. The high-floor Viewmaster, with taller windscreen and entrance/cab glazing, was added in 1977.

From 1980, the range was replaced by the Supreme IV (with more level windscreen) and updated Viewmaster, both with redesigned grille and square headlamps. GT models launched then have mesh, rather than slatted grilles, but Plaxtons also offered the new front ends to operators wishing to modernise older Supreme and Elite bodies, so be warned, all is not what it might at first seem.

In 1981, the Supreme V replaced the IV. It has a flat, single-piece shallow rear window and larger tail lamps. It was accompanied by the Supreme VI, Plaxton's answer to the Duple Dominant III — with flat, shallow side windows for long distance work.

Above:

Plaxton Viewmaster: The GT-specification grille and Supreme IV headlamp layout are used on this DAF MB200. It also shows the pointed windscreen effect used on early Supremes. Many older coaches, like this one, have Northern Ireland or cherished number plates to disguise their age.

Below:

Plaxton Supreme: A Supreme VI-bodied Volvo B10M with shallow side windows for long-distance work.

Plaxton Paramount

Built: Scarborough, North Yorkshire.
Chassis: Bedford Y-Series, VAS; Ford R-Series; Leyland Tiger, Royal Tiger; Volvo B10M, B9M; DAF MB, SB; Scania K92, K93, K112, K113; ACE Puma; Mercedes-Benz O.303; Neoplan N722; Quest 80 VM; Dennis Dorchester, Javelin.

The Supreme and Viewmaster were succeeded in 1982 by the Ogle-designed Paramount built as the 3.2m 3200, 3.5m 3500 and 4m 4000. The 4000 was launched as a double-decker in 1984 and as a 1½-decker with rear saloon in 1985.

It has the bowed sides first used in the Elite, but has square-edged windows. On the 3200 and 3500, a short 'feature' window was fitted behind the first main side window on most models, with the window line then sweeping down to meet the deeper windscreen. The 3200 has a single-piece windscreen, the 3500 a taller, horizontally-divided one. For 1985, the Mk II version introduced optional bonded glazing and an optional low driving position with a horizontally-divided windscreen on 3200 models. The three-axle 4000 double-decker, built first on Neoplan underframes, later on Scania and DAF chassis, has bowed top deck windows and its lower deck windows sweep up towards the front to clear the front wheelarch. The 4000RS 1½-decker, on three-axle Volvo B10MT chassis, has a window line which sweeps down behind the back axle.

For 1987, the Ogle-restyled Mk III, with bonded glazing only, moved the 'feature' window on the 3200 and 3500 to be a deeper five-sided design immediately behind the entrance/cab. The grille was re-designed and horizontally-divided windscreens became standard, with the top raked back on the 3500. National Express bought 3500-bodied B10Ms, badged Expressliner, in 1989-91 with an unglazed rear with large double-N symbol and white logos on the top corners of the windscreen. Production of the 3200 and 3500 ended in 1991, but the 4000 was kept to meet limited demand.

Below:
Plaxton Paramount: A Mk I Paramount 3500-bodied Leyland Tiger, with horizontally-divided windscreen and 'feature' window behind the front axle. The offside Continental door is at the rear of this coach.

Plaxton Paramount: A newer Paramount-bodied Tiger, in 3200 form, with repositioned 'feature' window and restyled grille.

Below left:
Plaxton Paramount: Rear view of one of the Expressliner 3500 coaches with side lockers and unglazed rear end and showing the deeper cab window on the higher version of the body. The rear section is moulded in plastic and can be replaced by a glazed section when the coaches are sold. Most Expressliners are leased to express service operators by National Expressliners Ltd, a company owned jointly by National Express and Plaxton.

Bottom left:
Plaxton Paramount: A Paramount 4000 double-decker on a DAF SB3000 chassis, showing the swept window line over the front axle. The 4000 was the first 4m double-deck coach from a British manufacturer.

Plaxton Premiere and Excalibur

Built: Scarborough, North Yorkshire.
Chassis: Volvo B10M; Scania K93, K113; Dennis Javelin.
The first totally new Plaxton coach range in 23 years was unveiled in 1991. They have flat sides with tucked-in skirts, rear windows which curve into the roof, shallow, rectangular headlamp units and large plug-type rear boot lids on struts. Underfloor-engined chassis have a grille in the lower front dash, other vehicles a plain panel. The 3.2m Premiere and 3.5m Premiere 350 have an upright front; the skirt area is stepped down ahead of the front axle on the 3.2m, swept down more deeply in a curve on the 350 which also has a horizontally-divided windscreen. The top-of-the-range Excalibur has a raked front with a thicker pillar behind the entrance/cab. For export, a 3.7m version of the Excalibur, the Prestige, is built initially on Volvo's rear-engined B12R chassis not yet available in the UK. The Prestige has separate upper and lower windscreens.

Bottom:
Plaxton Premiere: The upright lines of the Premiere are apparent on this 3.2m model. The grille arrangement on underfloor-engined coaches is reminiscent of the Ikarus body imported by Plaxton's Kirkby dealership. The Premiere 350 has a horizontally divided windscreen and the skirt design of the Excalibur coach. *Plaxton*

Above:
Plaxton Excalibur: Although the main part of the body is identical to the Premiere 350, the Excalibur's raked front and thick front pillar transforms its appearance. The upswept skirt at the front is also used on the Premiere 350. *Plaxton*

Above:
Reeve Burgess: A Swift coach with Harrier body operating a hotel shuttle service at Heathrow Airport. Note the recessed area around the windscreen wiper mountings.

Reeve Burgess

Built: Pilsley, Derbyshire; Scarborough, North Yorkshire.
Chassis: Leyland Swift.

Reeve Burgess introduced the Harrier body on the Leyland Swift in 1988. It has gasket-mounted square-edged side windows and a large single-piece windscreen. The recessed area around the wiper mechanism creates an illusion of a deeper central section of the windscreen. There are a few bus versions of the Harrier, and larger operators include Hyndburn, Pennine Motor Services and Kingston upon Hull City Transport's York Pullman fleet.

Setra

Built: Ulm, Germany; Ligny-en-Barrois, France; Samano, Spain 1976 to date.
Engines: Mercedes-Benz OM422 V8, OM421 V6; Cummins L10; MAN D2866.
Transmission: ZF synchromesh.

The Setra integral coach (the name comes from German *selbst tragend*, meaning 'self-supporting') is built by Kassböhrer and has been imported regularly to the UK since 1981. The 3.4m-high V6-engined S210HD (8.9m and 12m) and S215HD (12m with V8 engine or Spanish-built, MAN-engined Tornado) coaches have bowed sides, bonded glazing and curvaceous front and rear windscreens. The S228DT Imperial six-wheel double-decker has a strong family resemblance, with a raked upper deck windscreen; the entrance door and cab windows sweep up to meet the top of the lower windscreen. The French-built S215HR Rational is a cheaper 3.3m V8 single-decker with front drum brakes instead of discs and either gasket-mounted or bonded glazing.

Below:
Setra: A short S210HD operated on London tourist duties by Capital Coaches, a subsidiary of the National Car Parks group.

Above:
Setra: A French-built Rational S215HR with gasket glazing and opening window vents.

Smit

Built: Netherlands.
Chassis: DAF MB, SB.
A few Smit-bodied DAFs were imported from 1982 to 1985. All have flat sides, but there are differences in the front end styling. Some have upright fronts, while the later Orion design, which is deceptively similar at first glance to the LAG Galaxy, has a raked front and single-piece windscreen.

Below:
Smit: An Orion body, with lines not unlike those of the LAG Galaxy, but with a less dramatically shaped windscreen.

TAZ Dubrava

Built: Zagreb, Croatia, Yugoslavia.
Engine: Mercedes-Benz OM422 V8.
Transmission: ZF synchromesh.

Over 60 Dubravas were imported between 1988 and 1990, filling the gap in the market left when Bova replaced the Europa with the Futura. Unlike the Charisma, this Yugoslavian import bears no outward resemblance to the Mercedes O.303. There are two versions, the 3.2m 3200 and 3.5m 3500, both with bowed sides, a single-piece windscreen and a passing hint of the Setra S200's shape.

Below:
Dubrava: A 3200 Dubrava with glazed offside Continental door. It also has an offside cab door.

Unicar

Built: Catoria, Spain.
Chassis: Bedford Y-Series; Volvo B58.

Imports of Unicar bodies in the late 1970s brought in a style with identical curved windscreens and back windows, flat, round-edged side windows, the frontmost of which is deeper, and a roofline which steps up behind the cab/entrance.

Above:
Unicar: A Unicar-bodied Volvo B58 operated by Skills of Nottingham.

Van Hool

Built: Lier, Belgium; Sargossa, Spain; Dublin, Ireland.
Chassis: AEC Reliance; Bedford Y-Series; Ford R-Series; Leyland Leopard, Tiger, Royal Tiger; DAF MB, SB; Mercedes-Benz O.303; Volvo B58, B10M, B9M; Scania K-Series, N112, N113; Dennis Lancet; ACE Puma; Integrals.

After selling small numbers of coaches in the UK in the early 1970s, Van Hool imported 300-Series bodies from 1975 from Belgium and the short-lived Van Hool-McArdle plant in Dublin. These use the large curved windscreen, shallow roofline, and grille/headlamp layout of the earlier designs, but had bowed sides with gasket glazing and rounded windows. From 1978, they were followed by the Spanish-built Aragon with square-edged side windows, restyled grille/headlamp layout and a shallow back window.

The similar T8 range of bodies and integral coaches, extending from 3.2m single-decker to 4m double-decker, replaced the Aragon from 1980. It is available with high or low driving positions and options of divided or single-piece windscreens. Most common T8 in Britain is the 3.4m and 3.6m Alizée, built as a separate body and as the T812 10m integral with MAN D2866 vertical rear engine. Others in the range are: 3.4m T815 Alicron and 3.6m T815 Acron integrals with MAN D2866, Cummins L10 or 11.6 litre DAF engine; 3.9m T818 Astron 1½-deck integral with mid underfloor MAN engine; 4m Astral 1½-deck body on Volvo B10MT three-axle chassis; 4m T824 Astromega double-decker with Mercedes-Benz OM422 V8 engine; and 4m Astrobel double-deck body on three-axle DAF SB3000 or Scania K112/K113 chassis.

Above right:
Van Hool: The Van Hool 300 body has curved sides and round-edged windows. This is a Bedford YMT with Dublin-built body.

Right:
Van Hool: An Alizée-bodied DAF operated by Shelton-Orsborn. The window above the offside Continental door is shallower than the others.

Van Rooijen

Built: Montfoort, Netherlands.
Chassis: DAF MB, SB; Volvo B10M.
Van Rooijen (pronounced 'Van Royen') Odysee bodies are among the most distinctive — and rare — on Britain's roads. They were first imported in 1983 and are identifiable by their flat sides, sharply raked windscreen, raked-forward rear end and forward-sloping pillar starting just behind the front wheels.

Below:
Van Rooijen: Flat sides and raked lines identify the Van Rooijen Odyssee body on this Volvo B10M. *Adrian Pearson*

Volvo C10M

Built: Biel, Switzerland 1984-86.
Engine: Volvo THD100.
Transmission: ZF synchromesh or automatic.
Ten of Volvo's short-lived high-specification 3.4m integral C10M coaches were imported to Britain. The underframe is Swedish, the body built under licence by Ramseier & Jenzer, a Swiss urban bus builder. Its bow-sided shape is distinguished by a short front overhang and long wheelbase designed to accommodate more luggage space. In common with the B10M, it has a mid-engine, but it is just ahead of the rear axle, again leaving more space for luggage accommodation.

Above:
Volvo C10M: Viscount Central, the coaching subsidiary of Burnley & Pendle Transport, operates two of the 10 C10Ms in Britain. Note the very long wheelbase and short front overhang.

Willowbrook

Built: Loughborough, Leicestershire
Chassis: Bedford Y-Series; AEC Reliance; Leyland Leopard, Tiger; Seddon Pennine 7; Ward Dalesman.

Willowbrook tried to make itself into a third force in the UK coach market, alongside Duple and Plaxton and ahead of the wave of Continental imports which struck in the late 1970s, when it launched the 008 Spacecar in 1974. It has the bowed sides of the Dominant and Elite, but the side windows sweep up to meet a shallow rear window. The front end has a shallow grille and an almost hexagonal windscreen (sometimes divided vertically). Most were built for NBC subsidiaries on Bedford and Leyland chassis.

Below:
Willowbrook: A 008 Spacecar body with upswept side windows and hexagonal windscreen.

Left:
Willowbrook: A 003 body on a Trent Leyland Leopard, part of a large NBC order for this body style.

Below left:
Willowbrook: A reconditioned Leopard fitted with a new Crusader body for the Mackie's of Alloa fleet. Mackie's operates several Willowbrook-rebodied vehicles and in 1991 took delivery of a Crusader body built on the last Ward Dalesman chassis. *Murdoch Currie*

The 008 Spacecar was replaced in 1979 by the 003, a prototype of which had already been built on a Seddon chassis. It looks more of a Duple/Plaxton clone, losing the upswept side windows and having Dominant I front and back windows. Most were built for NBC with the last orders being placed in 1980.

After it was reformed under new management, Willowbrook launched its new Crusader in 1985, initially on Bedford and Tiger chassis, later more common on rebodied chassis. The 3.3m Crusader has bowed sides, flat, gasket-mounted side windows, a single-piece windscreen and slightly raked front.

Wright

Built: Ballymena, Co Antrim.
Chassis: Bedford Y-Series; Leyland Tiger; ACE Puma; Ford R-Series.
The Wright Contour coach, developed from the TT bus body, was developed in co-operation with General Motors' styling department and, when launched in 1982, was only available on Bedford YNT chassis. Its appearance anticipated the Plaxton Excalibur, having a raked front with a deep curved windscreen, a deep glazed entrance door and thick pillar behind the cab/entrance. The high side windows have round edges disguised to look square. As an option, the rear wheels can be boxed in. Most Contours are 11m and 12m, but 8m versions were built on Puma and short Ford chassis.

Below:
Wright: A Bedford Venturer with Wright Contour body. This one has been rebuilt with a wheelchair lift at the back.

PART 4 MINIBUSES

Most urban minibuses and midibuses are developed from mass produced vans and light trucks, although there also are purpose-built vehicles. The smaller vehicles are usually converted from an existing van body. Consequently, this section concentrates more identification on the vans from which those vehicles are based, rather than the bodies, but gives more detail of the coachbuilt bodies on the larger vehicles. Minibus fleets have been transferred around the country quite frequently, making it difficult to list with any certainty where to expect to see particular types.

CHASSIS AND BASE VANS

Ford Transit

Built: Southampton, Hampshire 1965 to date.
Engines: Ford diesel or petrol.
Transmission: Ford synchromesh or automatic.
Bodywork: Carlyle, Dormobile, PMT, Mellor, Alexander, Robin Hood, Rootes.
Britain's most popular van became the basis of the first minibuses bought in 1984/85. These were converted from Dormobile parcel vans, usually as 16-seaters, later 20-seaters. Most have large rectangular side windows, but Carlyle bodies have smaller, more round glazing.

A completely new Transit, with windscreen and bonnet integrated into a sharply raked front, was launched in 1986 after most operators had moved on to larger minibuses. Dormobile and Mellor have built bus versions, with Transit Holdings using substantial numbers on its services in Portsmouth, Oxford and Devon.

Below:
Ford Transit: A 16-seat Carlyle-converted old model Transit in the Cambus fleet.

Above:
Ford Transit: A Mellor-bodied 16-seat new-type Transit operated by Transit Holdings' Blue Admiral fleet in Portsmouth.

Freight Rover Sherpa

Built: Birmingham 1985 to date.
Engines: Land Rover, Perkins or Ford diesel.
Transmission: Synchromesh.
Bodywork: Carlyle, Dormobile, PMT, Optare, Robin Hood, Elme

Long and short wheelbase versions of the Sherpa, developed by Austin Morris in the early 1970s and most recently built by Leyland DAF as the DAF 200 and 400, enjoyed a short burst of popularity as urban minibuses when the switch to the new Transit created a shortage of suitable vehicles. Earlier versions are adapted from the Dormobile parcel van and have deep front quarterlights not fitted on the Transit. Later Carlyle and PMT bodies have more angular coachbuilt bodies. Some Sherpas have been rebuilt with Transit engines and gearboxes.

Below:
Freight Rover Sherpa: The later, more angular Carlyle body on a Sherpa run in Great Yarmouth by Flying Banana.

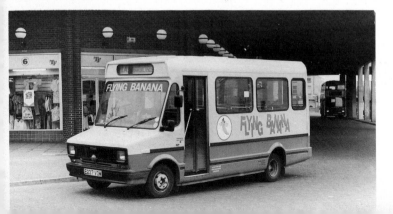

Iveco Daily: A later Daily 59.12 with a Cromweld-structured Carlyle body. Note the different grille design. *Iveco Ford Truck*

Iveco Daily

Built: Brescia and Suzzara, Italy 1978 to date.
Engine: Iveco diesel.
Transmission: Synchromesh or automatic.
Bodywork: Robin Hood, LHE, Phoenix, Carlyle, Dormobile, Reeve Burgess, Mellor, Car-Chair.
The Daily bus is based on the 40.8 4.2-tonne, 49.10 5-tonne, 49.12 5.2-tonne and 59.12 6-tonne light trucks. It is supplied as a chassis/bonnet cowl upon which bodybuilders fit appropriate bodywork up to 28 seats. Pre-1989 models have flat grilles and round headlamps; later models have a more pointed bonnet with a smaller grille between square headlamps. Some bodybuilders disguise the bonnet with their own design.

Below:
Iveco Daily: An older model Daily, bodied by Carlyle, in the Leicester CityBus fleet. Although built in Italy, it carries Iveco and Ford badges as the UK sales company, Iveco Ford, is owned jointly by the two companies.

Mercedes-Benz Transporter ranges

Built: Dusseldorf, Germany 1967 to date.
Engine: Mercedes diesel.
Transmission: Synchromesh or automatic.
Bodywork: Alexander, Dormobile, Reeve Burgess, PMT, Robin Hood, LHE, Phoenix, Europa, Optare, Wright, Carlyle, Wadham Stringer, Crystals.
NBC companies, in particular, were keen late purchasers of the T1-range L608D van which was available with a factory-installed bus back on its van body. As a 20-seater, it represented the first step ahead of the 16-seat Transit. It is identifiable by the single-piece windscreen with quarterlights. The successor T2 range, launched in 1986, is most common as a chassis/cowl with coachbuilt bodywork, but some have been converted from vans. Buses are based on the 609 5.6 tonne, 709 and 711 6.6 tonne, and 811 and 814 7.2 tonne van chassis.

Above:
Mercedes-Benz: A Milton Keynes City Bus L608D with van body converted by Alexander.

Below:
Mercedes-Benz: A Crystals-converted 709 operated by Fairline Coaches on a Scottish Citylink shuttle between Glasgow and Glasgow Airport.

Renault (Dodge) S56, S75

Built: Dunstable, Bedfordshire.
Engine: Perkins.
Transmission: Synchromesh, Chrysler or Allison automatic.
Bodywork: Alexander, East Lancs, Northern Counties, Reeve Burgess.
The Renault light truck began life as the Dodge 50 and many of the earlier bus versions are badged as such, often also with Renault diamond logos. Like the Iveco, they are supplied as chassis/cowls with a raked windscreen, although some bodybuilders have fitted their own bonnet arrangements. The S56 is a 6-tonne 25-seater; the S75, a 33-seat 7.5-tonner designed for bus operation. London Buses is one of the larger operators of S75s.

Talbot Express Pullman

Built: Coventry, West Midlands 1986 to date.
Engines: Sofim diesel, PSA petrol.
Transmission: Synchromesh.
The six-wheel Pullman is a UK-engineered version of the Italian-built Express van, a joint Fiat/Peugeot product. Its small wheels and front-wheel-drive give it a low floor only 20in from the ground. The Pullman name is from an old Humber limousine built by Rootes whose business is now owned by Peugeot. In 1990, production rights were sold to TBP of West Bromwich.

Above:
Talbot Express Pullman: A Western Scottish six-wheel Talbot used on special services for disabled people.

BODIES AND COMPLETE VEHICLES

Alexander

Built: Falkirk, Stirlingshire 1985 to date.
Chassis: Renault S56, S75; Mercedes 709, 811, 814.

Having converted some Mercedes vans to minibuses, Alexander developed its coachbuilt AM-type body for chassis/cowls. In its original form on Renault S56 chassis, it has a shallow windscreen, low-set side windows and a heavy-looking roof. Later models have high-set windows which meet the roof and taller windscreens with a wider destination box. Both designs have deep quarterlights. Side windows can be square or round-edged.

Below:
Alexander AM: The early version of the AM, as on this United Auto S56, has the side windows set in line with the shallow Renault windscreen. This creates an almost top-heavy look.

Above:
Alexander AM: The later version of the AM, most common on Mercedes T2s, has a taller windscreen and shallower roof. This is an 811 in London Buses' Centrewest fleet. Stagecoach companies operate 100 with high-set round-edged windows on shorter 709 chassis.

Below:
Carlyle: A Cambus Mercedes 811 with the body style developed partly to challenge the London Buses market.

Carlyle

Built: Birmingham 1989-91.
Chassis: Mercedes 811, 814; Iveco Daily.
Carlyle's 33-seat body has flat sides, square-edged bonded glazing and a square destination box which stands proud of the front roof dome. The Carlyle name is moulded into the offside of the back end. The last body, a prototype for the Iveco 59.12, was built using the stainless steel Cromweld system used on the Dartline body. Production rights have been bought by Marshalls of Cambridge.

CVE Omni

Built: Shildon, Co Durham 1988-90.
Engines: Land Rover or Perkins diesel.
Transmission: ZF synchromesh.
The integral Omni, with front-wheel-drive, air suspension and low floor is an Austrian Steyr design manufactured by City Vehicle Engineering, a company set up to build the bus. It was too late into the market to sell well to major bus fleets, but proved more popular in the welfare market. CVE went into receivership in 1990, shortly after a longer six-wheel Omni was developed. A successor company, Omni-Coach, was formed in 1991 to sell the vehicle. It has a heavily raked windscreen with flat glass; some shorter models have no rear overhang.

Below:
CVE Omni: The low floor of the Omni makes it attractive for mobility services, including London Transport's inter-station Carelink. *Stewart J. Brown*

Dormobile

Built: Folkestone, Kent 1985 to date.
Chassis: Mercedes L608D, 709, 711, 811, 814; Renault S56; Iveco Daily.
Dormobile, famous for the motor caravans it has long since ceased to build, built a square design of body on Renault and Iveco chassis, but in 1989 replaced it with a bow-sided design with deep quarterlights. An adapted version, retaining the original windscreens, was used by Milton Keynes City Bus to rebody two of its L608Ds in 1990.

Below:
Dormobile: One of the more unusual minibus projects has been Milton Keynes City Bus's modernisation of Mercedes L608Ds by fitting wider Dormobile bodies. The body uses plastic mouldings and uses the original windscreens of the 608. Dormobile has also bodied new vehicles to this style, but with taller windscreens.

Europa

Built: Doncaster, South Yorkshire 1989-91.
Chassis: Mercedes-Benz 609, 709, 811; Renault S75.
Europa developed from van conversions into the coachbuilt midibus market in 1989, when ex-MCW and Reeve Burgess staff joined the small company. The Enterprise bus body has a square-cornered windscreen, rounded roofline and destination box recessed in the front dome. Enterprise was bought by PMT and Brighton Buses, but the company collapsed in 1991. A successor, Autobus Classique, resumed production soon after.

Above:
Europa: A Europa-bodied Mercedes 709 operated by City Traveller in Hull.

Northern Counties

Built: Wigan, Greater Manchester 1986 to date.
Chassis: Renault S56.

Northern Counties was one of the first traditional bus builders to diversify into minibuses, starting with a utilitarian van-like body married to the standard S56 bonnet and windscreen. This was replaced by a design with a taller, arched windscreen (incorporating destination display) and cab windows which slope sharply to meet the small quarterlights. In 1988 this body was replaced by a design with a separate destination display, a disguised bonnet, larger quarterlights and level window line; it was named Countybus Pageant in 1992.

Below:
Northern Counties: The second design of Northern Counties minibus, on a Greater Manchester Buses Renault S56, with the swept-down cab windows and tall windscreen.

Above:
Northern Counties: The later minibus body, also on Renault S56, partly conceals the bonnet assembly. This one is operated by Cleveland Transit.

Optare City Pacer

Built: Leeds, West Yorkshire 1986 to date.
Chassis: Volkswagen LT55.
The City Pacer set the trend for rake-fronted minibuses. It was styled by Leeds art students and based on a 5.5-tonne Volkswagen van not normally sold in the UK. The chassis, with synchromesh or Allison automatic gearbox, is rebuilt with a higher driving position set back behind, rather than over the front axle, and with outriggers added to take bodywork with seats four abreast. The side windows stop short of the roof. Bus versions have two-leaf doors and a deep rear window, Inter-City Pacer coaches a single-leaf door and shallow rear window.

Optare StarRider

Built: Leeds, West Yorkshire 1987 to date.
Chassis: Mercedes-Benz 811.
As changing demands began to leave the City Pacer behind, Optare developed the larger StarRider on the Mercedes 811. The bonnet/cowl assemblies are discarded and replaced by a shallower windscreen and quarterlights than on the Volkswagen. There are buses and coaches and in 1990 an economy version with Mercedes bonnet and windscreen, the SRe, was offered. London Buses operates large numbers of StarRiders.

Above:
Optare City Pacer: The City Pacer body, with deep raked windscreen, is wider than the Volkswagen van chassis.

Below:
Optare StarRider: A StarRider operated on an Oxford-Milton Keynes service.

Above:
MCW Metrorider: A short MCW-built Metrorider, with divided windscreen, in the Yorkshire Rider fleet. Note the upswept rear window and bonded glazing.

Below:
Optare Metrorider: A narrow, long wheelbase Optare-built Metrorider, operated by Ipswich, with gasket glazing and straight side windows.

Optare (MCW) Metrorider

Built: Birmingham 1986-89; Leeds, West Yorkshire 1989 to date.
Engines: Cummins 6B, Perkins Phaser.
Transmission: Allison or Chrysler automatic, ZF synchromesh.

The Metrorider began life as an MCW product, the first urban midibus designed as such from the outset. Styling was influenced by the Optare City Pacer, but the windows reach almost to the roof. MCW achieved extraordinary success in selling it, in 7m (up to 25 seats) and 8.4m (up to 33 seats) lengths, 2.2m and 2.4m widths and as a bus and a coach. They went to many large fleets, including London Buses, West Midlands Travel, Strathclyde Buses, Cardiff Bus and several NBC companies, but MCW lost money developing it and its success ironically contributed to the company's decision to close. Optare bought the design, beefed up the mechanical specification (standardising on Cummins engine and Allison gearbox) and simplified the body. Most narrow Optare vehicles have single-piece windscreens and all have short aluminium side panels instead of stretched steel sections, StarRider-style glass fibre skirts, gasket instead of bonded glazing and straight side windows in place of the upswept rear window on the MCW version. Optare does not build a coach, but has sold buses to Ipswich, London Buses, Wilts & Dorset, SMT, Newport and Reading, as well as to several smaller StarRider customers.

PMT Ami

Built: Stoke-on-Trent, Staffordshire.
Chassis: Mercedes-Benz 811.

PMT followed the raked-front trend in 1989 with the Ami which has sold mostly to the PMT bus company. It has shallow side windows, an integrated destination box and windscreen and a thin grille intake between the headlamps.

Below:
PMT Ami: The Ami shape is influenced by Optare, but the windscreen is more upright and the glazing extends to the roof.

Reeve Burgess

Built: Pilsley, Derbyshire; Scarborough, North Yorkshire.
Chassis: Mercedes T2 range; Renault S56, S75; Iveco Daily.
Reeve Burgess is the leading minibus builder on the UK market and its products have been built at Plaxton's Scarborough factory since the Pilsley works closed in 1991. An earlier design with round-edged windows gave way in 1987 to the Beaver, which has square-edged gasket-mounted windows and a destination box built into the full width of the front roof dome. The Beaver is available in different lengths and widths, as a bus and a coach. Large customers include London Buses, South Yorkshire Transport, Yorkshire Traction, the Badgerline group, Devon General, SMT and Plymouth Citybus.

Below:
Reeve Burgess: A wide-body Beaver on a Mercedes 709 chassis in the Badgerline group's Thamesway fleet.

Robin Hood/Phoenix/LHE/CarChair

Built: Fareham and Eastleigh, Hampshire; Hailsham, East Sussex.
Chassis: Iveco Daily; Mercedes-Benz T2 range.
Robin Hood developed from small-scale minicoach building into one of the suppliers of converted minibuses for NBC in the mid-1980s. It then developed the popular City Nippy 21 and 25-seat body for the Iveco Daily range. It has a tall windscreen with integrated destination display and shallower side windows, usually round edged. It developed a larger body for Mercedes chassis, with slightly higher set side windows and a more arched roof. Coach and occasional bus versions have a curved windscreen which conceals the bonnet. The company changed hands in 1989 and became Phoenix International, but founder Robbie Hood formed the rival LHE Vehicle Engineering at Eastleigh, building similar designs of bus. Both companies have since closed, but Hailsham-based CarChair supplied eight Iveco 49.10-based buses to Solent Blue Line in 1992.

Above:
Robin Hood: A City Nipper-bodied Iveco Daily in Transit Holdings' Red Admiral fleet in Portsmouth.

Below:
Robin Hood: The later Robin Hood body style on a Milton Keynes City Bus Mercedes-Benz.

Wadham Stringer

Built: Waterlooville, Hampshire.
Chassis: Mercedes-Benz 709.
Wadham Stringer has been a more minor player in the minibus market. The Wessex body, with round-edged windows and arrow-shaped quarterlights, is operated by Brighton & Hove (vehicles supplied new to Bournemouth), Plymouth Citybus and Buffalo Travel in Bedfordshire.

Below:
Wright: A Wright-bodied Renault S75 of London Buses.   *R. J. Waterhouse*

Wright

Built: Ballymena, Co Antrim.
Chassis: Renault S75, Mercedes-Benz T2.
Wright's midibuses use the same Alusuisse construction system as the larger bodies in its range. They have the same round-edged thick rubber window mountings as the Handybus body on the Dart and have a destination box which is raised above roof level. London Buses, Midland Red South, Stevensons and Ulsterbus operate Wright midis; some Ulsterbus vehicles have full fronts with the bonnet concealed within larger quarterlights.